Current approaches to collective bargaining

Labour-Management Relations Series No. 71

Current approaches to collective bargaining

An ILO Symposium on Collective Bargaining in Industrialised Market Economy Countries (Geneva, 2-6 November 1987)

International Labour Office   Geneva

Copyright © International Labour Organisation 1989

Publications of the International Labour Office enjoy copyright under Protocol 2 of the Universal Copyright Convention. Nevertheless, short excerpts from them may be reproduced without authorisation, on condition that the source is indicated. For rights of reproduction or translation, application should be made to the Publications Branch (Rights and Permissions), International Labour Office, CH-1211 Geneva 22, Switzerland. The International Labour Office welcomes such applications.

ISBN 92-2-106503-0
ISSN 0538-8325

First published 1989

The designations employed in ILO publications, which are in conformity with United Nations practice, and the presentation of material therein do not imply the expression of any opinion whatsoever on the part of the International Labour Office concerning the legal status of any country, area or territory or of its authorities, or concerning the delimitation of its frontiers.
The responsibility for opinions expressed in signed articles, studies and other contributions rests solely with their authors, and publication does not constitute an endorsement by the International Labour Office of the opinions expressed in them.
Reference to names of firms and commercial products and processes does not imply their endorsement by the International Labour Office, and any failure to mention a particular firm, commercial product or process is not a sign of disapproval.

ILO publications can be obtained through major booksellers or ILO local offices in many countries, or direct from ILO Publications, International Labour Office, CH-1211 Geneva 22, Switzerland. A catalogue or list of new publications will be sent free of charge from the above address.

Printed by the International Labour Office, Geneva, Switzerland

Foreword

This volume of the Labour-Management Relations Series reproduces a selection of the documents that were submitted to a Symposium on Collective Bargaining in Industrialised Market Economy Countries, held in Geneva from 2 to 6 November 1987, with a view to promoting an exchange of views and experiences about recent trends and problems in collective bargaining in the countries concerned.

The Symposium convened by the ILO was attended by 140 participants from government, employer, worker and academic circles of the following countries: Australia, Austria, Belgium, Canada, Cyprus, Denmark, Finland, France, the Federal Republic of Germany, Greece, Ireland, Israel, Italy, Japan, Luxembourg, the Netherlands, New Zealand, Norway, Portugal, Spain, Sweden, Switzerland, Turkey, the United Kingdom and the United States. Observers from the Organisation for Economic Co-operation and Development (OECD), the Commission of the European Communities, the International Organisation of Employers, the International Confederation of Free Trade Unions, the World Confederation of Labour and the World Federation of Trade Unions, also attended the Symposium.

The first part of this volume contains the papers presented to the Symposium by the ILO and an analysis of the discussions held. The second part includes a number of documents submitted by the participants. For financial reasons, it is only possible, at this stage, to publish a selection of the contributions submitted in English. It is hoped that it will be possible to publish, at a later stage, a number of the contributions submitted in French. In any case, all the contributions submitted to the Symposium, whether in English or French, are available on request from the Labour Law and Labour Relations Branch of the International Labour Office.

Contents

Foreword v

Part One. Documents prepared by the ILO

Collective bargaining in industrialised market economy countries: Background paper prepared by the ILO 3
Introduction to the discussions, by A. Pankert, Head, Labour Management Relations Section, Labour Law and Labour Relations Branch, ILO 17
Analysis of the discussions, by A. Gladstone, Director, Industrial Relations and Labour Administration Department, ILO 25

Part Two. Written contributions of participants

Collective bargaining in Australia: Recent trends and problems, by B. Yates, Principal Adviser, Wages and Incomes Policy, Department of Industrial Relations, Canberra 35
Collective bargaining in Austria: Recent trends and problems, by the Federal Ministry of Labour and Social Affairs, in co-operation with the Austrian Congress of Chambers of Workers, the Federal Economic Chamber, the Confederation of Austrian Trade Unions, and the Association of Austrian Industrialists 45
Collective bargaining in Ontario, Canada: Recent trends and problems, by V. Pathe, Assistant Deputy-Minister, Industrial Relations Division, Ministry of Labour of Ontario 53
Collective bargaining in Denmark: Recent trends and problems, a joint paper by government, employer and worker participants from Denmark 61
Collective bargaining in Finland: Recent trends and problems, by T. Kallio, National Conciliation Officer, Ministry of Social Affairs and Health 71
Collective bargaining in the Federal Republic of Germany: Recent trends and problems, by W. Koberski, Department of Labour Law, Federal Ministry of Labour and Social Affairs 75
Collective bargaining policy in times of change: Developments in the Federal Republic of Germany, by Dr. K. Dutti, Chief Executive Officer, Federation of Employers in the Private Banking Sector and Dr. P. Knevels, Executive Officer, Confederation of German Employers' Associations 81
Collective bargaining in the Federal Republic of Germany: Recent trends and problems, by Mr. J. Kreimer de Fries, German Confederation of Trade Unions (DGB), Department of Collective Bargaining Policy of the Confederation's Executive Committee 93
Collective bargaining in Italy: Recent trends and problems, by T. Treu, Professor of Labour Law at the University of Pavia 97
Collective bargaining in Japan: Recent trends and problems, by T. Nakamura, Assistant Minister for International Affairs, Ministry of Labour, Tokyo 105
Collective bargaining in the Netherlands: Recent trends and problems, by H.J. Brouwer and Mrs. L. Kootstra, Ministry of Social Affairs and Employment, in co-operation with J.K. Bout and J.W. Van Den Braak, General Association of Employers, Netherlands Employers' Federation 113

Collective bargaining in New Zealand: Recent trends and problems, by B. Hill, Director, Employment Policy, Department of Labour ... 119

Bargaining systems, income policies and conflict in the Nordic countries, by Professor Nils Elvander, the Swedish Council for Management and Work Life Issues ... 127

Collective bargaining in Norway: Recent trends and problems, by K. Groholt, Director-General, Ministry of Local Government and Labour, Oslo ... 137

Collective bargaining in the United Kingdom: Recent trends and problems, by Mrs. A. Mackie, OBE, FIPM, Employee Relations Adviser, Unilever UKCR Ltd., London ... 147

Collective bargaining in the United States: Recent trends and problems, by H.C. Spring, Executive Assistant to the Deputy Under Secretary for Labor-Management Relations and Co-operative Programs ... 153

Collective bargaining in the United States: Recent trends and problems, by O.M. Sherman, Retired Vice-President, Goodyear Tyre and Rubber Company ... 161

Appendix. List of participants and observers ... 165

Part One

Documents prepared by the ILO

Collective bargaining in industrialised market economy countries

Background paper prepared by the ILO

This Symposium provides an opportunity to exchange views and experiences on general trends and problems in collective bargaining in recent, as well as in coming, years. The Symposium will take stock of the situation – ten years after the Symposium held in Vienna – in the light of the past decade's economic constraints, technological innovations, structural adjustments and changes in the employment market. The Symposium is not expected to adopt conclusions, resolutions, recommendations or other instruments.

When the ILO Governing Body approved the Symposium at its 235th Session (November 1986), it did not establish a detailed agenda but merely noted that the Symposium would consider such questions as the effects of economic, technological and social developments on workers' and employers' organisations, the role of the State in collective bargaining, and the level and substance of collective bargaining.

This document has been prepared by the ILO to facilitate the Symposium's discussions. It does not pretend to give a detailed description of the law and practice on collective bargaining in the countries attending the Symposium. Instead, with the aid of a few examples, it simply attempts to define general trends and problems that have been observed in the area of collective bargaining. It does not address issues proper to the public service, except in so far as they affect bargaining in the private sector.

1. The context

Industrial relations in industrialised market economy countries are currently evolving in a particularly difficult context. Three main factors seem to account for this: the economic problems which have beset these countries for the past 15 years, the rapid pace of technological innovation (it being understood that these two factors have brought about some structural changes in the economies of the countries concerned) as well as changes in the composition of the labour force and in the attitudes of wage and salary earners.

The economic problems of industrialised market economy countries are well known; there is no reason to elaborate the subject. Suffice it to note that in most of these countries industrial relations stand against a backdrop of slow economic growth, high unemployment that shows no sign of falling significantly, and relentless competition. Competition, in particular, has in some cases led to the deregulation of domestic markets, which in conjunction with the growing participation of developing countries in world markets has compelled enterprises to strive for even higher levels of efficiency.

Technological progress, spearheaded by micro-electronics, has also had repercussions on industrial relations, as exemplified by the vanishing distinction between blue-collar and white-collar workers, the growing number of skilled technicians, and the need to undertake major reforms in the organisation of work at the level of the enterprise.

Economic constraints and technological innovations have brought about a number of changes in the structure of the economies; these changes, in turn, have not been without consequence for industrial relations. Particularly noteworthy developments include the compression and restructuring of several branches of the manufacturing industry, the rapid expansion of the tertiary or services sector, and the proliferation of small and medium-sized enterprises, sometimes set up by former employees and most conspicuous in the high-tech sectors, where they often act as subcontractors for larger enterprises.

Changes in the composition of the labour force and in the attitudes of wage and salary earners can be traced in part to economic circumstances and technological developments; but they also respond to their own dynamics. Economic difficulties and technological progress have, for example, modified the structure of the labour force – particularly its distribution by level of skills – and have fostered an increase in "precarious" or "atypical" forms of employment, such as temporary work, part-time work, short-term contracts of employment and subcontracting. The "precarisation" of employment is creating an increasing division in the labour market between a stable core of workers and a number of marginal groups with quite a different fate. Foremost among the changes resulting from the internal dynamics of the labour force is the massive entry of women into the labour market. There have also been significant changes in attitudes: a number of women and young persons, among others, are showing a preference for life-styles in which wage employment occupies a less important and less constraining place than in the past; this attitude often contributes to the spread of "precarious" forms of employment. Certain wage earners have also shown a tendency to place greater reliance on their own efforts, rather than on collective action, as a means of furthering career development. Clearly, these changes have led to a more heterogeneous labour force which employers find more difficult to manage, which trade unions find more difficult to organise and which the public authorities find more difficult to regulate.

2. The repercussions of economic, technological and social developments on workers' and employers' organisations

The economic, technological and social developments outlined above have had a number of repercussions on trade unions. The most frequently cited is the decline in union membership. No doubt, the extent of this phenomenon has often been overstated. This is perhaps due to the fact that many analysts have been too strongly influenced by the situation in the United States, where the fall in union membership has been more pronounced than elsewhere. According to the AFL-CIO, less than 19 per cent of the workforce was unionised in 1985, compared with 35 per cent in 1954.

At any rate, it is true that there has been a tendency since the late 1970s for union membership to fall in a number of countries (e.g. France and the United Kingdom), due in large measure to the decline of sectors which have traditionally been among the more highly organised: trade union gains in service industries and in the public services have not been able to offset these losses. It must be noted, however, that trade union membership has remained stable, and even increased slightly, in other countries (e.g. Canada and Sweden). These contrasting developments have not been sufficiently analysed, though the question certainly seems to merit serious consideration.

Above and beyond the question of declining membership, there are other, more fundamental, problems which are unlikely to disappear as the current economic "crisis" recedes. They are closely related to the above-mentioned changes in the composition of the labour force and in the attitudes of workers. It may, for example, be asked whether the internal structure of trade unions adequately reflects the blurring distinction between blue-collar and white-collar workers or the growth in the number of skilled technicians. Trade unions are also having difficulties in attracting certain new categories of workers, such as highly skilled technicians, or "precarious" or "atypical" workers.

Given the diminishing influence of a number of trade union organisations, it is little wonder that certain employers have found it easier than before to avoid dealing with them (especially in countries such as the United States, whose system of industrial relations lends itself more readily to this attitude), or that certain governments have taken measures which effectively limit the freedom of action of trade unions (for example, several Acts adopted in the United Kingdom in the 1980s specifically sought to introduce restrictions on closed shops and direct action).

Nor is it surprising that trade unions have lost some of their strength at the bargaining table. And yet, workers' as well as employers' confederations have retained a great deal of influence in central tripartite dialogue, at least in countries with strong tripartite traditions, and continue to work closely with government in matters involving major social and economic decisions. It would be interesting to investigate why the weakened position of certain trade unions in collective bargaining (in the strict sense of the term, i.e. the negotiation of bilateral or trilateral agreements) has not necessarily been accompanied by a loss of influence in the social dialogue with the public authorities.

Of course, trade unions are very much aware of the problems cited above and have given much thought to ways in which the situation might be remedied. Since it falls clearly within their competence to define their own strategies in these areas, this document does not seek to enter into the debate but will simply mention some of the more commonly asked questions. Should trade unions strive to remain, first and foremost, the defenders of the collective interests of workers vis-à-vis employers and the government, and foster as great a solidarity among workers as possible? Should they, while still placing the greatest emphasis on the defence of the collective interests of workers, adopt a variety of approaches which would lead to a more specific treatment of the various sectors, enterprises and categories of workers? Should they concentrate their efforts on offering to individual workers, including non-unionised workers, a broad range of services (for instance, legal advice, vocational training, credit, insurance)? Should they conceive of their basic function in terms of the adoption of protective legislation for workers and the supervision of its application? Should they essentially try to influence government and encourage it to devise – at the national and international levels – economic, financial and trade policies that will, in the opinion of the trade unions, guarantee an orderly return to stronger growth, broader employment opportunites and greater social justice?

In their own way, employers' organisations are also faced with the need to make certain adjustments owing to changes in the profile of their current and potential members. Their challenges, however, would appear to be less dramatic than those confronting the trade unions. The most frequently cited problem concerns the swelling ranks of small and medium-sized enterprises, especially in services and the high-tech sector; this has added a new dimension to a traditional problem of employers' organisations, namely, the difficulty of attracting smaller enterprises and integrating them into their organisation.

Lastly, the decentralisation of collective bargaining, typical of the Western European experience in recent years, might – if it continues – have a significant impact on the internal structures of employers' and workers' organisations, and on their roles and functions at various levels (inter-occupational, sectoral, local, etc.). This question will be explored in greater detail in section 4.

3. The role of the State in industrial relations

Since the onset of the recession in 1973, the governments of many industrialised market economy countries have tended to take an increasingly active part in collective bargaining, especially in connection with the fixing of wages, whenever it appeared that the social partners might not reach an agreement, or that such agreements might be incompatible with the requirements of national economic recovery as perceived by the public authorities.

Sometimes following precedents which predated 1973, the governments of certain countries (e.g. Australia, Italy and Spain) influenced the outcome of collective bargaining by participating in inter-occupational tripartite agreements that sought to define comprehensive solutions to problems as varied as employment, remuneration, taxation, public expenditure, and social security and labour legislation reform. It will also be noted that the Austrian approach to social dialogue, which was instituted in 1957, continued unchanged through the "crisis" years, even though it has not been completely free of problems in very recent times.

In other countries, particularly those where tripartite discussions have run into major difficulties, the government has appropriated some of the social partners' prerogatives and intervened in negotiations by imposing measures aimed at settling outstanding issues. In some countries (e.g. France) such government measures have been highly selective and time-bound, as typified by wage freezes lasting no more than a few months. In other countries (e.g. Belgium and Denmark) the government's action has consisted of prolonged and massive intervention on matters traditionally settled though collective bargaining.

While the State's role in industrial relations has grown in some countries, elesewhere governments have adopted a different posture. In some countries, governments have traditionally avoided any direct intervention in collective bargaining (e.g. the Federal Republic of Germany and Switzerland); in some other countries, where such forms of intervention have not been altogether unknown in the past, governments have systematically avoided intervening in more recent years, in keeping with the policy options of current administrations (e.g. the United Kingdom and the United States); in still other countries governments, after years of deep involvement in collective bargaining, have recently tried to change course (e.g. the Netherlands).

These divergent attitudes reflect the hesitation of the governments of industrialised market economies as regards their role in social and economic matters. Nevertheless, it is evident that the State's intervention in industrial relations has in many countries assumed proportions that would have been unthinkable in the early 1970s. It would also appear that, apart from temporary measures taken in exceptional circumstances, the State's intervention in collective bargaining ill suits the political, social and economic context of industrialised market economies, and that its effectiveness decreases the longer it lasts. Does this mean that the more extensive forms of intervention are not likely to survive?

It should be recalled that certain restrictions imposed by the governments of industrialised market economy countries on collective bargaining have raised a number of problems as regards the compatibility of such restrictions with the relevant ILO standards. It would seem that, from the standpoint of principle, these governments continue to endorse the standards in question, but consider that they are unable to apply them fully at the present time. What should be the response to this situation?

4. The structure of collective bargaining

The structure of collective bargaining is determined essentially by the level at which negotiations take place. In this connection, the industrialised market economies have experienced several important developments in the past ten years. Notwithstanding certain exceptional cases (such as that of Australia, where industrial relations have again been centralised within the framework of a voluntary incomes policy promoted by the Government), there has been a trend towards the decentralisation of bargaining in the majority of the countries concerned. This is certainly true of most Western European countries, where bargaining structures had been quite centralised for several decades, and also of other countries where bargaining, although traditionally decentralised, has become even more fragmented in recent years (for example, in certain industries in the United States).

This section will focus on the European countries, since developments in their bargaining procedures are the most striking ones. By the early 1970s most European countries had for quite some time relied on a fairly complex model of bargaining in which negotiations at the industry or sectoral level continued to occupy the most important place, it being however understood that bipartite or tripartite inter-occupational negotiations as well as enterprise negotiations were also playing a certain role in many countries.

In recent years inter-occupational negotiations have lost ground and enterprise-level bargaining has expanded. Bipartite inter-occupational negotiations have been temporarily suspended in countries where they were most firmly rooted (e.g. Denmark, Norway and Sweden). Whether bipartite or tripartite, inter-occupational negotiations have run up against problems in other countries, leading either to temporary suspension or provisional or definitive abandonment of such negotiations (e.g. Ireland, Italy, the Netherlands and Spain). The difficulties currently besetting inter-occupational negotiations can be traced to the employers' wish to avoid the costs that often result from inter-occupational agreements, and to their fear that rules set at the highest level will prove too rigid. Moreover, some workers favour a more decentralised approach to bargaining whenever they have reason to believe that they stand to gain more than they would from high-level negotiations. In addition, as regards more particularly tripartite negotiations, budgetary constraints have diminished the government's ability to offer employers and workers the kinds of advantages that they require as a *quid pro quo* for the concessions they are expected to make. In these circumstances, it is easy to understand why inter-occupational negotiations, where they still exist, are generally less far-reaching, but on the contrary, more limited and flexible than they used to be (e.g. Belgium and Sweden).

In conjunction with the diminishing importance of inter-occupational negotiations, there has been a very clear trend in most Western European countries towards enterprise-level bargaining (e.g. France, the Federal Republic of Germany, Norway and the United Kingdom). In some cases company agreements must respect the rather narrow frameworks established by branch agreements (as exemplified by the reduction of working hours in the Federal Republic of Germany in 1984); elsewhere, the parties' freedom of action at the enterprise level is not impaired by sectoral agreements. The trend towards the decentralisation of collective bargaining is largely explained by the fact that certain questions of structural adjustment – such as the safeguarding of employment, the increases of productivity and the introduction of new technologies – can only be resolved adequately at the level of the enterprise. Moreover, many employers are convinced that only enterprise-level bargaining can offer the flexibility needed in the organisation of production.

It is impossible to say how far the decentralisation of collective bargaining in Western Europe will go. One of the most important questions in this regard is whether the extension of enterprise-level bargaining will ultimately lead to the disappearance of inter-occupational and even sectoral negotiations. Such a prospect would imply fundamental changes in the system of industrial relations in western European countries. Traditionally, the social partners in these countries have endeavoured to institute negotiations at the lower levels, within frameworks established at higher levels, thus ensuring a certain degree of control over general social and economic developments. In other words, sectoral and inter-occupational bargaining has been the price that the social partners have been willing to pay in order to avoid what they perceived as the risk of anarchy in industrial relations. The experience of recent decades seems indeed to confirm that high-level negotiations – and tripartite inter-occupational negotiations, in particular – have often helped to stabilise the social and economic situation of European countries over relatively long periods of time, but lead to important agreements which have defined widely accepted solutions to the major social and economic problems of the moment. To what extent are European governments, employers and workers ready to abandon this approach?

Barring a reversal of these trends, the continued decline of inter-occupational negotiations and the flourishing of enterprise-level bargaining might have significant consequences for the employers' and workers' organisations of the countries concerned. In particular, negotiations would escape the influence of upper-level organisations, to become the province of lower-level organisations (and – on the employers' side – of individual employers), thereby eroding the influence of central or sectoral organisations (and – on the employers' side – of regional and local organisations). Are European employers and workers prepared to accept such radical changes? If so, will they compensate for the loss of influence in collective bargaining on the part of these organisations by, for instance, entrusting to them the provision of more individualised member services in such areas as management consultancy, occupational training and retraining?

On an entirely different level, it should be noted that the growing recourse to enterprise-level bargaining has often raised problems regarding the relations between trade unions and bodies such as the works councils commonly found in European enterprises. The negotiation of wages and other important conditions of employment, such as hours of work, has traditionally been considered the exclusive prerogative of trade unions; but, works councils have always had a tendency to assume some of the bargaining functions which legally or theoretically belong to the trade unions. As the number of issues to be settled at the enterprise level increases – which, as suggested above, has been the case recently in Western Europe – the relations between works councils, or their equivalents, and the trade unions have become more problematic. To what extent has the decentralisation of collective bargaining resulted in a strengthening of the role of the trade union within the enterprise in European countries? Assuming that works councils in certain countries have in fact tended to assume some of the trade unions' traditional prerogatives, what would be an appropriate response?

Beyond the question of the level of collective bargaining is the broader question of its structure; a growing number of problems have been encountered in certain countries as regards the place of the public service within this structure (e.g. in Canada, Italy and Sweden). There was a time when the public service was a relatively unimportant entity, at least in comparison with the private sector; furthermore, it represented a "separate" entity, since the status of civil servants was generally very different from that of workers in the private sector, in areas such as the right to bargain collectively, the right to strike, the security of employment as well as the levels and systems of remuneration. In these circumstances collective bargaining and joint consultations in the public service, if any, had no links with negotiations in the private sector.

In the past 15 to 20 years, the number of public employees has vastly increased in nearly every country, and collective bargaining – or other forms of collective dealings – has spread considerably in the public service of many countries. The net result is that the status of public employees in such countries has become much more akin to that of workers in the private sector. This trend has slowed in recent years, as many governments have had to adopt austerity policies and to take steps to halt the expansion of the public service, and to limit or even reduce wages in that sector. These steps have led to serious disputes in many countries. Today's public service has found strength in numbers; it is confident enought to seek to protect and enhance its situation as regards employment and income; in addition, economic constraints have placed it in competition with the private sector (since funds allocated by the government to the public service are no longer available to the private sector, e.g. for creating new jobs or subsidising social security). For all these reasons, it would perhaps be advisable to establish some co-ordination between public service and private sector bargaining; the need for such co-ordination is clearly felt in some countries (e.g. Sweden), but the ways and means have yet to be defined.

5. The substance of collective bargaining

The most important current issues in collective bargaining are employment, the cost of labour, the flexibility of the labour market, the introduction of new technologies and the reduction of working hours. These are obviously not unrelated issues. Employment and the cost of labour are particularly entwined, and one of the major concerns of negotiations in recent years has focused on the need to moderate the escalating cost of labour, and even to freeze or reduce it, with a view to saving as many jobs as possible, and perhaps to create new ones. In this spirit, many of the earlier mechanisms used to tie wages to the cost-of-living index have been curtailed or even abolished in a number of countries (e.g. Denmark and Italy); such measures have sometimes been accompanied by stipulations requiring that funds thus "saved" be used, in part, to create new jobs, possibly though reductions in the hours of work (e.g. Belgium and the Netherlands). Of special interest is the bargaining which has taken place for several years in the United States on the questions of job security and the cost of labour. During an initial stage, which lasted from the late 1970s to the early 1980s, workers made concessions regarding the cost of labour in negotiations known as "concession bargaining", especially in the automotive and steel industries. Under the ensuing agreements they forfeited a number of established or future advantages, most often in connection with wages, in exchange for guarantees of job security and a greater degree of participation, which was usually expressed in terms of the trade unions' right to receive information on the company's financial situation. More recently, the improved economic situation of certain companies has led to the signing of agreements that call again for moderate wage increases and other advantages, and contain very sophisticated provisions concerning job security (e.g. the 1984 Ford and General Motors agreements and the 1986 Saturn agreement).

Another of the social partners' current concerns is the flexibility of the labour market. The employers and many governments believe that greater labour market flexibility would lead to substantial new hiring; in support of this argument, European employers and some European governments often cite the cases of the United States and Japan, claiming that they were able to create more new jobs than the European countries because their labour markets are more flexible. In general, the advocates of greater flexibility take a very broad approach to the subject, and this may explain why the term flexibility has acquired several meanings. When flexibility concerns the cost of labour, it designates either its adjustment on the macro-economic level to economic fluctuations, or its adaptation on the micro-economic level to the enterprise's profitability. In other cases, flexibility may concern certain legal provisions or regulations which are primarily designed to protect workers as regards job security and hours of work. In still other cases, it concerns the geographic and occupational mobility of labour or the organisation of work, with all the implications that these issues may have in areas as diverse as vocational training, wage classifications and restrictive labour practices.

The first debates on flexibility took place in the early 1980s and were extremely difficult. The vagueness of the concept raised a number of difficulties, but the major problem was due to the employers' and certain governments' wholehearted defence of flexibility, on the one hand, and the trade unions' determined opposition, on the other. In fact, the trade unions saw flexibility essentially as an attempt to dismantle their social conquests of the past century – an attempt which capitalised on the shift in the balance of power which had taken place to the detriment of the workers. In these circumstances, the talks were generally more doctrinaire than substantive, and degenerated into a series of points and counterpoints which failed to convince anyone.

Although the current debate on flexibility is far from easy, there has been some progress in recent years, as indicated in the OECD's recently published "Dahrendorf Report".[1] Indeed the advocates of flexibility no longer view it as a panacea, and the trade unions are more willing to admit that in certain specific areas, the labour market may entail certain rigidities inappropriate to current circumstances. As a result, discussions have become more pragmatic. Everyone seems to agree that it is not possible to discuss the labour market's "overall" flexibility, but instead that each of its aspects must be examined separately; moreover, there seems to be a greater awareness that increased flexibility does not always lead to increased efficiency (for example, job security may have beneficial effects on workers' motivation; longer hours of work may diminish their productivity); what is more, there is a growing recognition of the need to weigh the economic effectiveness of certain measures under consideration against their social cost.

These developments in the general approach to the question of flexibility have made it possible to deal with some of its aspects through collective bargaining. This is especially true of working hours (for example, the agreement of 23 April 1986 signed by Belgium's National Labour Council opens up new possibilities as regards the daily limit of hours of work, work on Sundays and night work for women). In other areas such as job security, however, negotiations have generally failed; where measures have been taken in this connection, they have generally been the result of legislation (for

[1] OECD: *Labour market flexibility,* Report by a High-Level Group of Experts to the Secretary-General (Paris, 1986).

example, the 1986 repeal of the administrative authorisation for dismissals on economic grounds in France, and much national legislation which has expanded opportunities for temporary work and short-term contracts). As regards these two last issues, mention can however also be made of a few formal or informal enterprise-level agreements which limit the employer's discretion to have recourse to these types of work and which protect the workers in question in the areas of wages, working conditions and trade union membership (e.g. the United Kingdom).

There are two other important issues in negotiation, which though related to issues of flexibility, extend considerably beyond it; they concern the introduction of new technologies and the reduction of hours of work. Recognising the futility of any opposition on their part, trade unions have generally adopted a positive attitude towards technological progress and lent their support on the condition that new technologies be introduced in accordance with socially acceptable terms and conditions. Inter-occupational, sectoral and enterprise-level agreements in many countries have sought to define the general principles to be followed in introducing new technologies; these agreements generally stipulate that workers are to be notified in advance and are to participate, in one way or another, in decision-making as regards the social aspects of the innovations concerned. When specific technological innovations are introduced in a given enterprise, the employer and the trade unions often conclude agreements which not only aim at defining measures to be taken to protect the workers concerned, but also address the broader inter-related issues of increased productivity, improved quality of production, strengthening of co-operation within the enterprise as well as greater job satisfaction through greater worker autonomy and better conditions of work and life.

The reduction in hours of work has always been a prominent concern in negotiations, but it has acquired a new dimension since the early years of the "crisis". Trade unions in most countries have insistently demanded significant reductions in hours of work as a means of reducing unemployment. This objective is sometimes related to the broader aim of achieving a fundamental redistribution of working time and leisure time (as exemplified by individual retirement plans, sabbaticals, greater equality between the sexes as concerns responsibility for the home and wage-paying employment). In general, employers have not welcomed the reduction of the hours of work: they are convinced that measures to that effect would not significantly lower unemployment levels; moreover, given the current economic circumstances, they think that it would be very difficult to reduce the hours of work and maintain remuneration at current levels. In practice, there have been widespread, but moderate, reductions in working time. These arrangements are often accompanied by provisions allowing for greater flexibility in schedules. In many cases, the reduction of hours of work is part of an overall package of wage measures designed to lower its cost. Ultimately, however, developments in this area can be classified as "classical" approaches to the reduction of working time which have little effect on employment and fall far short of the more ambitious reforms mentioned above.

The most important conclusion to be drawn from the foregoing might be that collective bargaining, despite the difficulties and impasses it has encountered in industrialised market economies in the past decade and a half, has proved its ability to adapt: after years during which it was used as a means of continually and almost automatically improving the situation of workers on a quantitative level (for example, wage increases and related benefits, reduction of hours of work, etc.), collective bargaining is increasingly used as a tool to strengthen the competitive posture of enterprises and to guarantee the protection and enhance the situation of workers on a predominantly qualitative level (for example, through training and occupational recycling, job security, job satisfaction, flexible hours, etc.).

6. The climate of industrial relations: Disputes, co-operation and participation

Industrial relations in the industrialised market economies seem to show a tendency, in the 1980s, towards greater co-operation between the social partners. Although it is premature to speak of a fundamental and pervasive change, there are many signs that seem to confirm this trend.

The most important of these signs concerns the number of days of work lost to strikes and lock-outs. Although the number of disputes in the public service has risen in many countries, and despite a number of major disputes in other sectors (e.g. the miners' strike in the United Kingdom and the strikes over hours of work in the Federal Republic of Germany), statistics clearly show that in most countries the number of days of work lost as the result of labour disputes has diminished since 1980.

There have also been certain changes in the nature of collective bargaining itself. In many industrialised market economy countries, the growing number of appeals by employers and governments for greater co-operation at the bargaining table is matched by those of a number of trade unions which recognise the usefulness of negotiations in resolving current problems of structural adjustment. In practice, this has led to the changes in the nature and substance of negotiations which were discussed at the end of the previous section. It may also be noted that there are clauses for social peace in countries where they were practically unknown (for example, agreements concluded by the British subsidiaries of Japanese firms); moreover, profit-sharing and stock-option schemes have proliferated in may countries.

Also noteworthy is the development within enterprises of certain forms of participation which seek to introduce a variety of more or less informal arrangements for co-operation between management and labour with a view to improving the organisation of work and increasing productivity, particularly on the introduction of new technologies. These arrangements may take the form of participatory personnel policies, quality circles or standing advisory committees. It must be mentioned, however, that efforts have been made, in certain instances, to prevent the involvement of trade unions in these arrangements, frequently by restricting participation to works councils or similar bodies. But even these bodies are sometimes circumvented in an attempt to deal directly with the workers themselves. Where this has been the case, it is no longer impossible to speak of collective representation of workers: there is, at present, a shift of certain issues from the domain of collective relations to that of individual relations or, in other words, a shift from "industrial relations", which is essentially bilateral, to a form of "human resource management" which is essentially unilateral.

These trends as well as the reluctance of workers' representatives to participate in difficult decisions that have often to be made in periods of economic recession, help to explain why institutional participation has not made any significant progress recently in the industrialised market economy countries – especially in Europe – although such participation is traditionally well established and developed considerably in these countries from 1965 to 1975. While it is true that the advisory powers of works councils have been expanded in a number of countries, especially as regards the social aspects of the introduction of new technologies, there are virtually no developments worth pointing out as regards co-determination rights of works councils or worker representation on boards of companies. This situation is further underscored by the fact that, within the European Economic Community, neither the proposal for a fifth directive (concerning the structure of public limited liability companies and the powers and obligations of their statutory bodies), nor the proposed "Vredeling" directive (concerning procedures for informing and consulting the employees of undertakings with complex structures, in particular transnational undertakings) has come to fruition.

Lastly, although there seems to be widespread agreement among experts that a greater degree of co-operation has evolved within industrial relations, there is no unanimity in the interpretation of this phenomenon. Are we to believe those who say that this transformation is merely a by-product of the current economic situation, and that industrial relations will turn adversarial once economic activity picks up again? Or are we to believe those who say that we are witnessing fundamental and lasting changes in the attitudes of workers and management, in the sense that even significant improvements in the economic outlook would leave unresolved a whole set of problems that would call for co-operation between the social partners?

Final remarks

These final remarks are not "conclusions" in the sense that they do not purport to offer an overall diagnosis of the current situation of collective bargaining in industrialised market economies, much less to offer a prognosis or recommendations concerning its future. Rather, their aim is to explain why it seems premature to draw hard and fast conclusions.

One reason is that there are still no obvious trends as concerns the solutions to some current problems. For instance, there is no clear indication of how trade unions plan to approach the various problems facing them. Likewise, it is difficult to say whether the public authorities, which in some countries continue to intervene in collective bargaining and in others seek to curtail their involvement, will eventually adopt more accommodating attitudes and, if so, in what way.

Even where trends are clear, it is still difficult to draw conclusions because of the uncertainty over whether these trends will continue and, if so, to what extent. Thus, it is currently impossible to predict with any degree of certainty how important "precarious" or "atypical" employment will be in ten or 15 years, or for that matter, the average hours of work, or the degree of flexibility in work scheduling. Moreover, as regards industrial relations in the strict sense of the term, no one really knows to what extent bargaining will be decentralised ten or 15 years hence. Are we to believe those who say that "nothing will ever be the same as before", or those who foresee only "adjustments", even if such adjustments are relatively significant?

Introduction to the discussions

Alfred Pankert, Head, Labour Management Relations Section,
Labour Law and Labour Relations Branch, ILO

These introductory comments aim to review some of the current questions being asked about collective bargaining in industrialised market economy countries. I hope that these comments will allow participants to focus their discussions, at least to a certain extent, on these questions. It should, however, be clearly understood that this introduction in no way aims at imposing a restrictive framework on these deliberations and that participants are free to deal with all the matters that are of particular concern to them.

Since this Symposium is intended primarily to allow an exchange of views among participants, this presentation will be kept as short as possible. Consequently, I will touch upon a limited number of problems only and restrict myself to those which seem to be of major significance. Moreover, I will deal with these selected problems in a relatively summary manner, going no further than to draw attention to the similarities which seem to exist between various industrialised countries in respect to each problem. The task here is difficult. The difficulty stems first from the fact that any similarities that may exist never apply to all the countries in question. Furthermore, even if there are similarities, what we have is only similar situations but not identical ones. Admittedly, I may from time to time indicate that this or that problem is non-existent – or virtually non-existent – in a certain country or that it occurs in only very specific terms in another. However, this will not be enough to avoid oversimplification and, consequently, to do full justice to the specific features of various national situations. Throughout this week, the task of the Symposium will be to take the picture that I intend to sketch and make the corrections and provide the additional information necessary for the participants' respective countries.

Now that I have specified these riders, I will come to the body of what I intend to say.

I will not dwell on the context in which labour-management relations have to evolve at the present time. Participants certainly know this context better than anyone and are aware of just how difficult it is – in particular, in view of economic constraints, technical progress and various changes which are currently occurring in the composition of the labour force and the attitudes of the workers.

The first major problem that I would like to deal with relates to the difficulties of internal adjustment that employers and trade union organisations have had to face in the difficult environment just mentioned. These difficulties are, without doubt, less pronounced for employers' organisations than for trade unions. One major problem faced by employers' organisations seems to be that of absorbing into their ranks the increasingly large number of small and medium-sized enterprises. Another is the problem – at least in Europe – of decentralisation of collective bargaining, which I will return to later. If the employers participating in the Symposium consider that this way of presenting the matter does not adequately reflect the adjustment problems of their organisations, they will doubtless draw attention to the fact during the course of the discussions.

The problems of adjustment that face trade unions have been widely commented on and discussed over recent years. There has been much talk of the fall in union membership and the difficulties unions are experiencing in organising the growing number of workers of certain categories such as skilled technicians or "atypical" workers. Various commentators have stated that, unless the situation changes, the trade unions' position in society in general and at the bargaining table in particular will continue to weaken – especially in countries where the attitudes of governments and certain employers' groups are scarcely favourable to the union movement. Various people have also asked whether tomorrow's unions will not be very different organisations from the ones we know today – in that, it seems, their main activities would be in fields other than those that are common today; however, the ideas of these commentators on what tomorrow's trade unionism might be are not very clear and do not always seem to be based on very objective analysis.

A number of written contributions made to the Symposium by workers' participants – and a number of trade union publications as well – indicate that workers' organisations do not deny that they are confronted with a number of problems. However, it can also be seen from these documents that the situation is one on which it is very difficult to generalise. During the debates, trade union participants will no doubt provide the Symposium with a series of indications which will re-establish the true proportions of the problem. Their statements will show how the situation varies from one country to another, and may offer explanations to a number of surprising findings – for example that the level of trade union membership has fallen in the United States whereas, just across the border, in Canada, it has increased; or that the weakened position of certain trade unions in collective bargaining has not necessarily been accompanied by a loss of influence in the social dialogue with the public authorities. The workers' participants will, no doubt, also explain what the national statistics on union membership levels actually mean in each of their respective countries, what trends are reflected in the most recent statistics of this kind, what the unions have already done to improve the organisation of those categories of workers among whom the level of unionisation continues to be low, and what they plan to do in the future to achieve further progress in this field. The workers' participants may also wish to say how they themselves view the future of trade unionism. There are a number of questions to be asked in this respect and I will mention only two for the sake of example. First: Can we expect trade unions in the future to go further in the direction that a number of them already seem to be willing to take, that of giving more case-specific solutions than in the past to the problems of different sectors of the economy, different enterprises and different categories of workers? Second: Can we expect that the trade unions' traditional activities, i.e. defending workers' collective interests, will in future be supplemented by a series of new activities such as services to members in the fields of credit or insurance, etc. – it being understood, however, that defending workers' collective interests would obviously remain the unions' main and intrinsic activity?

Another matter on which I would like to say a few words is that of the role of the State in industrial relations and, more particularly, in wage fixing. In some industrialised countries, this role has remained an insignificant one; however, in many others, it has taken on dimensions which could never have been foreseen in the early 1970s. In certain cases, governments have not – at least formally – questioned the voluntary nature of industrial relations systems and have limited themselves to participating in tripartite agreements or to influencing bipartite bargaining, without taking any compulsory measures. In other countries, on the other hand, governments or parliaments have gone so far as to appropriate some of the social partners' prerogatives and have intervened in negotiations by imposing measures aimed at settling outstanding issues.

In a pluralistic democracy, the question of the State's role in labour-management relations is certainly a major one. In the past, the principle has always been that the State should avoid any coercive intervention in industrial relations other than where really exceptional circumstances justify such a step for short periods. This principle still seems to be accepted as such in all industrialised market economy countries including those where it has not always been observed in practice: when the public authorities intervene through coercive measures in collective bargaining or when employers' organisations or trade unions accept such intervention tacitly, none of them do so happily. But this does not deny the existence of a problem where there is a desire to maintain certain principles as such but where it proves impossible to avoid bending these principles significantly and for long periods in practice. Symposium participants, and especially those from countries where bargaining freedom has been considerably restricted by the public authorities, will perhaps like to speak on this subject.

There is another very simple – but nevertheless quite basic – question on the role of the State in industrial relations that participants may wish to deal with. This is why the public authorities in certain industrialised market economy countries have, so far, been able to refrain from coercive intervention frequently in collective bargaining whereas others have had to intervene in this way. The Symposium may also perhaps wish to look at why non-coercive governmental intervention – which is perfectly compatible with a market economy and which often takes the shape of tripartite central agreements – have been systematically avoided in certain countries whereas they have been sought after in others (and have, moreover, often had a stabilising effect on industrial relations).

I would now like to consider a number of questions about the level of collective bargaining. Major developments are currently taking place in this area – with the decentralisation of bargaining in a large majority of industrialised countries. This is certainly the case in most Western European countries where, for many decades, the bargaining structure has been quite centralised; however, this also applies to certain other countries such as the United States where bargaining, which has traditionally been decentralised, seems to have become even more fragmented over recent years.

Coming back to Europe, where the trend towards decentralisation is the most pronounced, inter-occupational negotiations – where they are practised – have lost ground, and enterprise-level bargaining has expanded, although the extent of these two phenomena varies considerably from country to country. Employers are usually in favour of this trend, mainly because they consider that enterprises must have a margin for manoeuvre to be able to adapt to the demands of very intense national and international competition. The trade unions have taken the attitude they have usually adopted in difficult economic times and have, instead, often preferred to negotiate at higher levels – but opinions are not unanimous on this point in all countries. The attitudes of governments have varied from country to country: in certain cases, they have attempted to achieve tripartite or bipartite central agreements; in other cases, they have allowed the decentralisation trend to take its course. Symposium participants may wish to review the arguments which, in their opinion, favour continuation of the current degree of centralisation in collective bargaining or which favour decentralisation of bargaining.

Nevertheless, this is a discussion which should not be too general. Everything does, in fact, depend on the degree of decentralisation that one has in mind. Here it should be emphasised that if decentralisation to the enterprise level were pushed much further than is currently the case in European countries, the outcome would probably be fundamental changes in the system of industrial relations in these countries. The level of bargaining is not just a mere technical feature of an industrial relations system. Depending on whether a system is highly centralised or highly decentralised, the whole philosophy of how to tackle labour problems will change. In Europe, the social partners have traditionally negotiated at higher levels because they wished to ensure a certain degree of control over general social and economic developments and because they wanted to avoid what they perceived as the risk of anarchy in industrial relations. Is it possible that European governments, employers and workers might one day be ready to abandon this approach?

It should also be pointed out that significant expansion in enterprise-level bargaining in Europe might have important consequences for employers' and workers' organisations in the countries concerned. If this were to happen, negotiations would increasingly escape the influence of central and sectoral organisations. Certainly, these organisations might compensate this loss of influence by offering new services to their members and a number of them already seem to be doing so to some degree. However, even if these organisations could maintain a certain volume of activity in this way, their role would nevertheless undergo fundamental changes. Is it possible that these organisations might one day make important moves in this direction?

Whatever the future extent of decentralisation of collective bargaining in Europe, the developments that have taken place so far in this field already seem to have raised problems at the enterprise level. It has been reported on several occasions that certain negotiating functions which were traditionally considered the prerogative of trade unions have been taken over by bodies of the works council type. Symposium participants may wish to report on their experience in this area and look at whether the extension of enterprise-level negotiation has been accompanied by a corresponding strengthening of the role of the trade union at this level.

Over recent years – both in Europe and elsewhere – industrial relations at the enterprise, plant or workshop level have led not only to the conclusion of collective agreements in the legal sense of the term but have also given rise to the appearance of a whole series of often highly informal mechanisms of participation between employers and workers. The main aim of these has been to improve work organisation and productivity – in particular when new technologies are being introduced. Typical examples are quality circles or various information and consultation mechanisms. Developments such as these form part of a trend towards greater co-operation in industrial relations which has asserted itself in recent years, at least in certain countries and certain branches of activity. However, on many occasions, there have been attempts in some countries to impede the involvement of trade union representatives – and bodies of the works council type, where they exist – in these participation experiences; this has led to various matters being moved from the area of collective labour relations towards that of individual relations. Symposium participants, especially those from employer and worker circles, may wish to give an insight into the true extent of this phenomenon and their view on this point – and in particular on its repercussions on collective bargaining. They may also wish to tell us whether they see the trend towards greater co-operation in industrial relations being due mainly to a fundamental change in the attitudes of the parties involved or primarily the outcome of the recent shift in the balance of power to the detriment of the workers.

Going beyond the question of the level of negotiation and dealing with the wider problem of the negotiating structure, I would like to raise a problem which has been having acute effects for several years now in certain countries: "horizontal co-ordination" between the negotiations involving various categories of workers such as blue- and white-collar workers in the private sector and, in particular, workers in the private and public sectors. Previously, the negotiations for each of these groups took place virtually independently, mainly because private sector white-collar workers and public sector workers had a very different status to those of private sector blue-collar workers. Over the years, the difference in status between the three groups diminished while, at the same time, the proportion of private sector white-collar workers and the public sector workers – especially civil servants – has risen markedly in number and therefore in power in comparison with private sector blue-collar workers. The question of the advantages of each group in comparison with the others has thus become a real problem for a certain number of countries. This problem of comparison exists in any case between the private and public sectors, and also between blue- and white-collar workers in the private sector in countries where the distinction between these two categories is still an established one. All this leads to tensions not only when establishing the chronological sequence of negotiations for the various groups but also – and in particular – in determining the content of the agreements that should be drawn up for each of them. Symposium participants from countries where this problem of the "horizontal co-ordination" of negotiations is a topical one may wish to review the situation for us.

To conclude, I would like to make a few comments on the substance of collective bargaining. To simplify somewhat, it may be said that workers are primarily concerned by the problem of job security and they often go for massive reductions in hours of work in order to reduce unemployment; employers on the other hand, are mainly interested in enhancing the competitive edge of their enterprises by making them more "flexible" or more "adaptable" in various fields – the most important of which are labour costs, the terms and conditions of the individual employment relationship and patterns of working hour schedules. I will not enter into the controversy on the advantages and disadvantages of reducing hours of work and of the various forms of "flexibility" or "adaptability", and more specifically on their ability to absorb unemployment – controversies which continue to be sharp even though, in certain respects, they are less so than at the beginning of the 1980s. Instead, I will do no more than rapidly point to certain facts concerning the results of collective bargaining. Numerous agreements have resulted in concessions by the workers on labour costs as a counterpart for guarantees on job security and new information and consultation rights. A large number of agreements have also established reductions (although rather limited) in working hours, while at the same time offering employers – and sometimes also employees – greater flexibility in arranging their working time. Many agreements have also been drawn up when new technologies have been introduced: these agreements are intended to protect workers against the negative social consequences of the implementation of these technologies, and often contain clauses intended to make the enterprise more competitive by means of reforms in work organisation, occupational mobility of labour, and job and wage classifications.

While collective bargaining has often proved successful in the various fields just mentioned, it has been used only rarely – and has usually failed – in determining how far use may be made of certain types of "atypical" work. Consequently, this question has usually been settled by legislation.

The conclusion that may perhaps be drawn from this overview of the substance of collective bargaining is that some major adjustments have taken place in recent years: after years in which collective bargaining was used as a means of continually and almost automatically improving the situation of workers from a primarily quantitative point of view (for example, wage increases, reduction of hours of work, or increase in the length of holidays), it is now being used increasingly as a tool to make enterprises more competitive and to guarantee and enhance the situation of workers from a predominantly qualitative point of view (for example, through job security, job satisfaction and vocational retraining). Symposium participants may wish to indicate whether this is a correct diagnosis and, if so, to tell us whether, in their opinion, this approach will be continued in the future.

These are the main points which I wished to make and I will not add any conclusions. Currently, as far as collective bargaining is concerned, we are in an era of such change that it would probably be premature to draw any conclusions. In certain areas, developments are still taking place in opposite directions in different countries. This applies, for example, to state intervention in collective bargaining, which continues to be very marked in certain countries while it is systematically avoided in others. Nevertheless, in other and far more numerous fields, developments tend to be taking a convergent trend but it remains virtually impossible to answer the very important question of how far these developments will be carried: what will be – or what should be – in ten or 15 years' time, the average hours of work, the degree of flexibility in work scheduling, the importance of "atypical" work or the degree of decentralisation in collective bargaining? Hazarding somewhat more of a generalisation, one might also ask what is the probable or desirable extent of this broad trend which seems to underlie a number of current developments, i.e. the trend of reacting to present difficulties by developing solutions that are less uniform and more case-specific than in the past, sometimes promoting approaches which are more individualistic rather than collective and, where necessary, moving certain questions out of the area of collective labour relations into that of individual relations.

Analysis of the discussions

Alan Gladstone, Director, Industrial Relations and Labour
Administration Department, ILO

1. The situation of the organisations

Trade unions have certainly been affected by the economic recession, by structural change – particularly the decline in certain industries – by the introduction of new technology, by entry into the labour force of new groups with different expectations and needs, and by other factors that have been mentioned during the course of our discussions. But the impact has been different on the various trade union movements: loss of membership *and* of influence; loss of membership *without* significant loss of influence; stability of membership – even increase – *with* loss of influence none the less; and no significant loss of either membership or influence. I think the discussion shows however that, by and large, trade unions are more in a defensive posture than they have been in the past. Even Mr. Kreimer de Fries (Worker, Federal Republic of Germany) found a weakening of the trade union position in the Federal Republic.

Membership loss, either in absolute terms or as a percentage of the workforce, has been felt in Australia, France, Italy, Japan, the United Kingdom, the United States and others. On the other hand, trade unions in Canada, the Federal Republic of Germany, Israel, Norway and others seem to have been able to maintain their numerical strength and, in certain cases, increase that strength. There are cases, perhaps best exemplified by *Israel* (although atypical, I grant) where membership is the key to a number of social services not available, or not easily available, outside the union; hence membership, in any event, does not suffer. This relates to the question, also raised in the discussion, of new benefits and services which unions can offer to attract members – which I will discuss later.

On the question of influence, there are cases, and I think Ireland was cited, where even though the union might have lost bargaining strength, their influence – or "clout" – with government may be unaffected, particularly with regard to friendly labour or social democratic governments.

Even where overall numerical losses are registered, unions may keep their proportional numerical strength and influence in a given industry. We were indeed given some examples where the number of union members in an industry went down less, proportionately, than the overall cut-back of workers – and the union ended up with a greater percentage of membership.

Another and somewhat distinct cause of problems for unions' – or at least traditional unions' – strength or influence seems to be the emergence of small independent or unaffiliated trade unions, sometimes composed of key personnel, which can influence and perhaps undermine collective bargaining patterns and programmes set by established unions; Norway has referred to this phenomenon but it would appear to be cropping up elsewhere as well. In this regard, mention was made of certain situations in which there is, regardless of numbers, a real increase in union power through their control of key jobs.

Another sometimes destabilising aspect of the trade union situation that has been brought up in different ways, as regards the Federal Republic of Germany and Sweden, among other countries, is the competition between white-collar and blue-collar unions. With the increase in white-collar workers, blue-collar unions may seek to move further into the white-collar field. I think Professor Elvander (Sweden) mentioned that in his view the predominantly blue-collar LO in Sweden was no longer a pillar of the industrial relations system owing to the significant increase in white-collar workers outside of the LO. Furthermore, the increased blurring of blue-collar/white-collar distinctions could exacerbate the problem or, alternatively, resolve it by providing an incentive for merging blue-collar and white-collar unions where they still exist separately.

Now, in regard to this question of the situation of trade unions, many participants – and not only from the trade union side – referred to an increase in hostility on the part of employers towards trade unions. Where this is the case, it is probably both a reflection of – and a contributing factor to – the defensive posture of the unions in a number of our countries. A more hostile employer attitude (which incidentally would be, at least on the surface, inconsistent with the much referred to change from a climate of conflict to one of co-operation in labour relations) is sometimes coupled with a less than friendly attitude of governments towards unions in terms of policies and practices, application of existing laws, or enactment of new legislation. Among others, the United States, the United Kingdom (particularly in view of recent legislation regulating union affairs and internal decision-making) and Denmark have been referred to in this regard.

What can unions do and what are they doing to improve their situation? Here participants came up with a number of ideas, not all of which are uncontested. One of these, and this seems to be contemplated or emphasised by many unions, is to increase services and benefits outside the collective bargaining sphere, including the provision of such services and benefits to members not covered by a collective agreement, and even perhaps to non-members. Examples include financial services, including credit cards, travel, life and other insurance, legal services or insurance and others. Trade unions in Australia, Canada, Finland, the United States and elsewhere seem to be moving strongly in this direction. Others have long provided a variety of services.

Some participants on the union side worried that emphasis on these sorts of activities could weaken a "true" trade union vocation, whether it be changing society or simply furthering the interests of their members through collective bargaining and legislative action. It was pointed out, however, that affording new and extended benefits and services did not preclude pursuing traditional trade union functions. In this regard the representative of the Canadian Labour Congress strongly emphasised that their increase in membership was due to increased militancy in collective bargaining, as well as aligning themselves with progressive social groups to advance common interests.

Organisational changes in trade unions could also help to strengthen their position. Here, mergers and unification of unions, either at the central or branch level, were cited in Australia (at the central level), Ireland, Israel, Japan, New Zealand (360 unions down to 240) and the United States. There are certainly others.

There was much discussion about unions drastically increasing efforts to organise a wider range of categories of workers – some new on the labour market – that have been difficult to organise or which have not yet been solicited. These are groups that have proliferated on the labour market and are cited as a cause of diminishing trade union strength or influence. Women, young workers, employees in high-tech operations, part-time, temporary, casual and other workers in precarious, atypical or non-conventional employment were all referred to in this regard.

Mention was also made of shifting emphasis from collective bargaining, where the trade union position may not be too strong, to the legislative area: attracting or winning worker interest and support through legislative advances in safety and health, tax relief, job security, industrial development and other matters, sometimes with employer support.

We must not ignore the situation of employers' associations. Among other things, increased decentralisation of collective bargaining, where it is taking place, as well as the proliferation of smaller, often highly specialised enterprises that are not always interested in joining employers' associations, were cited as raising problems for employers' associations. In fact, someone mentioned with particular reference to decentralisation, that this could call into question the very *raison d'être* of employers' associations (although a lobbying function would always remain).

Some employers' associations, and the Irish case was described, have increased their services to members, sometimes charging fees: services such as management consulting, training in industrial relations and collective bargaining, providing data bases. In fact it was pointed out that with decentralisation, and particularly for the benefit of small firms, guidance and instruction in industrial relations and collective bargaining were all the more necessary. Some questions were raised as to whether provision of services of the kind mentioned could not put employers' associations in competition with private firms – consultants and others – some of whom might even be their own members.

2. The role of the State

The discussions showed that there were many forms and degrees of government intervention or involvement in collective bargaining, or more generally in industrial relations. Total abstention is probably found nowhere.

The State often provides a legislative framework that gives the ground rules for collective bargaining. This may or may not be passive or neutral (e.g. in having an impact on the level of collective bargaining which in turn affects the relative balance of power between the parties).

Other forms of intervention cited were by nature "heavier": mainly incomes policies of a mandatory nature. Also mentioned were national inter-occupational accords – voluntary agreements that were tripartite (or bipartite but with strong government involvement) – and which usually covered a wide range of economic and social subjects.

Another form of state involvement is the promotional role, for instance the efforts of many governments (the United States Department of Labor is an example) to promote labour-management co-operation in industry.

There are a number of countries which insisted that their policy was one of non-intervention in the collective bargaining process which respected the autonomy of the parties. These included Canada, Cyprus, the Federal Republic of Germany, Japan, the Netherlands (in a turn-around since 1982), New Zealand, Spain, the United Kingdom and the United States (although some of these were contested). From the discussions, it appears that this non-interventionist stance referred largely to the absence of an incomes policy or of legislative intervention in wages and terms and conditions of employment. Indeed, in some of these countries there were voluntary accords, participated in or supported by the government, which in fact did have a strong influence on wage levels and related matters.

A number of participants, including Mr. Nakamura (Government, Japan) and Mr. Bourlard (Government, Belgium), emphasised that the State could not be indifferent to wage movements in its role as the protector of the public economic interest and in its mission to avoid economic and social disaster. I would, however, cite in passing the remark of Mr. Brouwer (Government, the Netherlands) who explained that wages were more in line with productivity growth during the recent "non-interventionist" period that in the period when there was direct and intensive government intervention. I would also cite the remark of one participant that intervention in the form of incomes policies bears a close relationship to the extent of inflation, and that inflation is now at a relatively low level in most of the countries concerned.

It was also pointed out that the interplay of public and private sector wage levels and determination, and the conflicts that this gives rise to, provoked government intervention.

I should mention here again, although it also is relevant to the discussion of structure and levels of collective bargaining, the various accords, sometimes referred to as social compacts, that were cited in our discussions. Two of the most discussed of these voluntary instruments of incomes policies – the British accord of some years ago and the much discussed Australian accord – were in fact bipartite, i.e. concluded between the Government and the trade unions; the employers were not a party, although there may have been acquiescence. Other accords – none, I believe, of so comprehensive a nature – are tripartite.

Accords, and other forms of what is now commonly called social concertation, in Cyprus, Israel, Italy and Norway, do involve agreed incomes policies and provide a context in which wage negotiations can take place. It would appear that more stringent, unilaterally imposed incomes policies, as they were known in the Netherlands, Belgium and other countries, have given, or are giving, way to freer collective bargaining – although sometimes within the framework of the broad peak agreements just referred to.

Another view expressed was that the State need not interfere with free collective bargaining, it having many other monetary, fiscal and other instruments to influence the ultimate results of collective bargaining.

As to substance, it appears that the various centrally negotiated national accords and compacts involve a series of trade-offs in return for wage restraint (including lessening the effects of wage indexation) by such measures as government tax relief, training programmes, insurance improvements and a variety of other measures which can be taken by the public authorities.

To return to the role of legislation versus that of collective bargaining, and leaving aside the role of the State to assure minimum protection, the view was expressed (by Mr. Pascré – Worker, France) that given the strong imbalance in the collective bargaining relationship, legislation was necessary to fill the gap or void and ensure the necessary conditions, benefits and protection for workers.

But there is legislation and legislation. Much comment was reserved for the recent British enactments which some participants – not only from the trade union side – saw as a new set of rules governing union affairs and action that aimed at – or resulted in – modifying or changing the balance of power between the parties (and, incidentally or not so incidentally, removing certain supposed rigidities in collective bargaining). But what of the question of trade union democracy and protecting the individual trade union member against certain acts of his or her trade union?

3. The structure and levels of collective bargaining

The big question on structure seemed to be whether indeed there is a trend towards decentralisation of collective bargaining – and if so, what were the implications of such a trend. The question is indeed very complex. Although the concept was not completely clear, most participants understood decentralisation to refer principally to a move in collective bargaining to the enterprise and plant levels. At the same time, others – in the Nordic countries and elsewhere – saw decentralisation as chiefly a move from centralised inter-occupational collective bargaining to branch or industry-level collective bargaining.

I think that although Mr. Stalport (Worker, Belgium) concluded that decentralisation was a myth, there is considerable evidence that it *is* taking place in a number of countries. At the same time, from the discussions, I gather that there is no mass movement, and that a certain degree of decentralisation to enterprise level does not preclude continued collective bargaining at industry (branch and central levels). Perhaps we are dealing with – at least in some countries – an extension of bargaining to additional levels rather than a shift from one level to another. Moreover, those who do not see any pronounced decentralisation nevertheless refer to the fact that new problems have to be dealt with at the enterprise level – implicitly through some form of negotiation-like procedures.

A number of participants did in fact see an increase in lower levels of collective bargaining than has previously been the case. Norway has cited (80 per cent of wage increases are now decided at local levels) as well as Greece and perhaps Finland (one of our Finnish colleagues cited the lack of flexibility in centralised collective bargaining); in France also, in response to the Auroux laws and in the United Kingdom, where in addition, we were told, multi-employer collective bargaining is on the decline. In Ireland, there appears to have been a significant decentralisation in bargaining from 1979 to 1987, although the move is back to central wage bargaining now. In the United States there seems to be some decentralisation in the form of a move away from pattern bargaining. Denmark notes a decentralisation from the central to the industry or branch level. Japan (already at enterprise level) reports no change. Although participants from the Federal Republic of Germany seem to indicate no change as well, I cannot but wonder if there is not an increase in wage bargaining activity by works councils.

As to the position of the parties on decentralisation, it has generally been favoured by employers as a means of adapting wages and conditions to local circumstances, i.e. greater flexibility. Some employers – and governments as well – would add that there are certain items that can only be negotiated at the local level, particularly some of the newer or more novel issues now increasingly becoming the subject of negotiations in some contexts: introduction of technological change, aspects of work organisation and the like. The possibility that in some cases, as noted by some of our trade union colleagues, the balance of power is more on the side of the employer at the enterprise level, is probably not alien to a certain employer preference for decentralisation.

Most of the trade unionists, particularly those in Europe, seem to plead in favour of industry-wide or even more centralised collective bargaining in the name of worker solidarity; also since they might not otherwise be able to bargain with small and medium-sized enterprises where they would not easily have a presence or access.

On the other hand there are employers, or employers' associations such as in Belgium, which do not advocate decentralisation and, sometimes together with trade unions, prefer to retain a measure of control from the top, to avoid what they perceive as possible anarchy in collective bargaining and in settlements. They also invoke the good of the national economy in support of retaining more centralised bargaining moves. Employers' associations have also indicated that to move to enterprise-level collective bargaining would put small and medium-sized enterprises at the mercy of strong unions and that they need the help and protection of the employers' associations to correct the balance of power.

Might there also be an element, in the position of the trade unions and in that of employers' associations, to oppose or play down decentralisation to defend their own positions – their own *raison d'être*?

As Professor Blanpain (Belgium) pointed out, the level may also depend on such factors as the size of the country, the structure of the parties to collective bargaining, the role of government as well as the relative strength of the parties.

But really, and this was stressed by a number of participants, it is not a question of "either/or". Indeed, we have seen from our debates that in the same country a certain decentralisation to the enterprise level has not led to the disappearance of top-level framework-type agreements, and in fact we have examples of co-ordinated bargaining at three levels (in Greece and during certain periods in Italy) and two-level collective bargaining elsewhere. However, some employers felt that this was costly, in terms both of the amount of time managers' and employers' had to spend on bargaining, and the practice of seeking material improvements at each level above and beyond that agreed upon at previous levels.

Multi-level collective bargaining in any case should avoid contradiction; it should be what the Italians used to call "articulated". Here there are choices, as was pointed out, between minima being negotiated at higher levels and being improved upon at local levels; or different levels treating with different subject-matters. An example is the United Kingdom where we were told different parts of the pay packet are involved at different levels of bargaining. Mr. Nilsson of the Swedish Employers saw everyday questions such as wage payments, shift work and the like being treated at local levels, and broad questions such as social insurance, matters of principle and procedures such as industrial democracy and the like being bargained at the higher or confederal level.

One additional complication evoked was the question of the interplay of multi-level collective bargaining and, where it existed, the peace obligation (i.e. an obligation not to strike during the term of a collective agreement). The problem described is one where a collective agreement was concluded at a higher level and collective bargaining at a lower level did not lead to agreement. If the peace obligation were in force, this would deprive the trade union of a means of pressure at that lower level.

4. The substance or content of collective bargaining

There seemed to be a general feeling that there had been both an increase in the number of questions subjected to collective bargaining and at the same time a tendency at present for somewhat more emphasis to be put on qualitative matters than on quantitative or wage-related matters. Nevertheless, a number of participants insisted that wages were still the main focus of collective bargaining. This was stated with reference to Ireland, Japan, Norway and the United Kingdom; and for Ireland and the United Kingdom we were told there is little else treated in collective bargaining!

On the other hand, the Federal Republic of Germany, Italy, Switzerland and the United States are among those countries where there appeared to be a marked shift to qualitative issues in collective bargaining. It was suggested by Mr. McAuley (Employer, Ireland) that any trend away from wage issues might have been helped by this being a period of relatively low inflation in many of our countries.

On the so-called qualitative issues, we were reminded that there are very few things that did not have a price tag; at least some of the "non-material" matters, Mr. Schnyder de Wartensee (Employer, Switzerland) reminded us, can cost in the long run.

What were some of the qualitative bargaining issues – both with and without a price tag? Among those cited were working time arrangements, security of employment, equality, introduction of technological change; co-determination and other participation issues; training and retraining; productivity questions, and perhaps above all a number of questions relating to "flexibility". On this last issue were included questions of geographical and occupational mobility, redundancy measures, work reorganisation and the like.

Voices were heard questioning the negotiability of some of these items; for instance questions involving technological change. In the United Kingdom there was no collective bargaining – or even consultation – except after its introduction. The employer participants from the Federal Republic of Germany insisted that the introduction of technological change was entirely a management prerogative.

The general issue of flexibility is the tough one. I noted that Mr. Hardmeier (Worker, Switzerland), as well as the Luxembourg trade unions, would not oppose flexibility automatically, but insisted that it had to be negotiated. I am sure this position would be taken by many other trade unionists.

It was also pointed out by some of the employer and government participants that not all flexibility issues were necessarily against the interests of the workers or trade unions; witness flexible working time or certain geographical mobility measures. But this meant that the buzz-word of "flexibility" had to be disaggregated for intelligent discourse or collective bargaining. A number of our trade union participants remained sceptical, feeling that virtually all types of flexibility were in the exclusive interest of employers and were retrogressive in terms of long-established social rights.

Government and employer participants stressed the need to enhance flexibility and facilitate technological change as essential elements of becoming or remaining competitive; indeed for the viability and survival of enterprise.

Finally, it was noted by Mr. Groholt (Government, Norway) and others that with decentralisation of bargaining structures and with increasing deregulation, more and more items would find their way to the collective bargaining table. British statistics, however, seem to indicate that since 1980 the scope of collective bargaining has diminished – fewer things are being bargained.

5. The climate of collective bargaining

One aspect of the changing climate of collective bargaining already discussed is that concerning "social concertation", including tripartite and bipartite accords at the highest level. A participatory climate of respect, mutual trust and co-operation would seem to be a prerequisite for successful negotiation at the peak level. (Perhaps this is one reason why we have not as yet witnessed any very consistent and sustained progress in this domain.)

Although Mr. Hardmeier (Worker, Switzerland) suggested a hardening and even polarisation of the parties in some respects, i.e. a change in the balance of power in favour of employers, there certainly seemed to be, according to the participants, a significant lessening of disputes and a trend to more co-operative and less conflictual industrial relations. Whether this comes about because of a genuine mutual desire to co-operate in order to meet the critical problems facing the social partners (including that of maintaining and enhancing "competitiveness"), or whether it is a reflection of a weakened or at least more defensive trade union movement, is a good question. I would conclude from the discussions that it is a healthy dose of the former with a touch of the latter, but this may be an optimistic interpretation.

It was reported to us that labour disputes, principally work-days lost to strikes (and perhaps lock-outs) are down in recent years in most countries: the Federal Republic of Germany (taking account of the lengthy working time dispute); Italy (in spite of painful problems of restructuring); Finland, the United Kingdom (less and of shorter duration); Luxembourg; France; Australia; the United States and, I am sure, many other countries.

However, it would appear that there is an increase in labour strife, as reported to us, in the public sector or public service. This is the case in Israel, Canada and other countries. Is this possibly because the public sector is not as directly involved in terms of competitivity and the struggle for viability and survival whether in foreign or domestic markets? Is it also possibly because in some countries the public service has become the prime target for government initiatives of wage restraint, thereby leading to a change in traditional disparities as between the private and public sectors?

Increased co-operation at the enterprise level is reflected in recent agreements and arrangements cited in the American automobile industry and perhaps an increase in more informal consultations and contacts in countries like the United Kingdom. But we were advised by some participants that trade unions sometimes feared a "hidden agenda" by employers and were suspicious of certain co-operative initiatives. The trade unions wanted to ensure that recognition of individual values was not at the expense of collective representation, that is, they wish to guard against an "individualisation" of labour relations that could ultimately call into question the legitimacy, role and functions of trade unions which Professor Blanpain (Belgium) referred to as a form of "unilateralism" (sometimes equated with "human resources management").

It also appears from the discussions that the current interest in co-operation and participation, certainly by employers, and probably by many trade unions too, is not so much an interest in institutional forms – board-level and works council types – but more on workplace participation.

Finally, and assuming that the present period is one in which industrial relations and collective bargaining are witnessing a climate of greater co-operation and less adversarialism, the question was raised as to whether, should the economic situation improve significantly, industrial relations would not, in a number of countries, become more conflictual.

Part Two

Written contributions of participants

Collective bargaining in Australia: Recent trends and problems

Mr. B. Yates, Principal Adviser, Wages and Incomes Policy, Department of Industrial Relations, Canberra

1. Introduction

The Australian industrial relations system is characterised by the operation of independent industrial relations tribunals established at the state and federal level to prevent and settle industrial disputes by conciliation and arbitration. In the federal sphere, the Australian Conciliation and Arbitration Commission (the Arbitration Commission) fulfils this task and to a large extent occupies a leadership position for the state tribunals. Because of the importance of the tribunal system, collective bargaining in Australia has been referred to as "three-cornered bargaining" – reflecting the fact that negotiations may take place with the assistance of the Commission or be influenced by the outcome of the tribunal processes. Legally enforceable industrial awards cover some 85 per cent of employees.

The early 1980s in Australia saw the breakdown of the centralised wage system based on indexation which had been established in 1975. There was a shift to industry-level bargaining which in 1982 resulted in a dramatic rise in hourly labour costs. Combined with the onset of international recession and a severe drought, wage outcomes contributed to the deepest recession in Australia since the 1930s. Inflation reached over 11 per cent and unemployment grew to over 10 per cent. A wage freeze, sponsored by Australia's federal and state Governments, was instituted by the industrial tribunals late in 1982 and operated until September 1983.

The February 1983 Statement of Accord negotiated between the Australian Labour Party and the Australian Council of Trade Unions (ACTU) committed a federal Labour Government and the ACTU to the implementation of a comprehensive prices and incomes policy. This encompassed a wages policy based on the return to a centralised system of wage determination based on wage indexation. The present Labour Government was first elected to office in March 1983.

The major commitments of the Accord were in relation to such matters as prices and incomes policy; industrial development; "social wage" issues such as social welfare and education expenditure; occupational health and safety; industrial democracy; and the role of the public sector.

In an attempt to develop national reconciliation and consensus, the Labour Government held a National Economic Summit Conference in April 1983 to allow representatives of unions, employers, government and community groups to contribute to the formulation of a programme of national reconstruction. An important function of the Conference was to set a negotiated framework for a social contract approach to wages policy. Substantial agreement emerged for a return to a centralised wage system, although employer groups opposed the concept of wage indexation.

In September 1983, the Commission re-established a structured centralised form of wage fixation based on the notion of prima facie full indexation related to price movements and periodic increases related to productivity improvements. Labour cost increases beyond these general increases were to be very small and subject to conformity with prescribed wage principles. Unions were required to give commitments not to pursue claims outside those principles as a condition to gaining access to the benefits of the centralised system. Such commitments were generally forthcoming and complied with. Through its National Wage Case Decisions since 1983, the Arbitration Commission has fulfilled the role of a mediator in the process of fashioning and maintaining a broadly consensus-based wages policy, with the periodic submissions of the parties, including governments, aimed at necessary revision of the system in response to economic and other changes.

In the view of the parties to the Accord, the wage system contributed substantially during the period 1983-85 to the achievement of strong economic and employment growth through the containment of labour costs pressures and greater industrial stability. In recent years, the wage system has been revised in response to the serious external problems facing the economy – the substantial depreciation of the exchange rate, the adverse balance of payments, the sharp deterioration in the terms of trade and the substantial rise in the external debt. These developments imposed the need to improve Australia's international competitiveness, productivity and economic performance and to achieve greater restraint in labour cost growth.

Initially, revision of the system took the form of discounting wage increases for the price effects of the depreciation of the Australian dollar. Concern for the effect of persistent discounting on continued union commitment to the system, however, resulted in the introduction of a new wage system as a result of the Arbitration Commission's March 1987 National Wage Case Decision.

The March 1987 Decision marks a significant change, not least because of its impact on the scope and practice of collective bargaining. Based on the submissions of employers, unions and governments the Decision established a new two-tier wage-fixing system which first involves the assessment in a National Wage Case of the maximum level of increase that can be sustained over a period of time having regard to the broad range of industrial, economic and social factors affecting the Australian economy. The Arbitration Commission then determines:

(i) the apportionment of that increase between a general increase to all workers (the "first tier"); and
(ii) the setting of a ceiling on the level of wage increases and improvements in employment conditions able to be pursued at industry or enterprise level, in accordance with a series of defined wage-fixing principles (the "second tier").

The two-tier system is designed to ensure overall wage restraint consistent with the external constraints imposed on the economy, to encourage improved productivity and efficiency and to provide a measure of protection for lower-income earners. Critical to the economic objectives of the system is to bring Australia's unit labour cost growth more into line with that of its trading partners.

A degree of controlled flexibility, with increased scope for local bargaining, is introduced through the second tier of the system. A critical feature of the second tier is the introduction of a new wage-fixing principle to encourage the restructuring of industry and greater efficiency focused at plant and enterprise level. The "Restructuring and Efficiency Principle" gives expression to the general consensus reached between the parties in late 1986 on the need for provisions to promote the reform of restrictive work and management practices, the removal of demarcation barriers, the introduction of multi-skilling and new training arrangements for industry. The Commission expects that primary emphasis will be given to negotiations under this Principle.

The Commission's March 1987 Decision also established a new wage-fixing principle to provide for the inclusion of supplementary payments in industrial awards in order to assist lower-paid workers within occupations. Occupational superannuation has also emerged as a significant industrial issue in recent years. Provision is made in the system for certain superannuation arrangements to be established or improved through negotiation, with arbitration (on a phased basis) available where the parties are unable to negotiate a satisfactory outcome and where conciliation fails.

2. The operation of the two-tier system

Australian wage fixing has traditionally been highly centralised with negotiations taking place at the national, industry or sectoral level, rather than at the level of the company or plant, and tending to be co-ordinated or synchronised. A long period of the application of centralised wage indexation (1975-81, 1983 to March 1987) – with limitations on other sources of wage increases – has continued this trend, minimising local negotiations. While the two-tier wage system still retains the centralised National Wage Case as a key element, more decentralised bargaining, albeit within parameters determined centrally, is fostered through the second tier of the system.

Negotiations under the Restructuring and Efficiency Principle are occurring in most industries, although to date only a small number of agreements have been finalised, covering about 10 per cent of the workforce, but including some significant industries. Some common trends have begun to emerge, however, both from the finalised arrangements and the negotiations still in progress.

A significant number of second-tier negotiations have included measures to enhance flexibility in the use of labour, reduce restrictive work and management practices, improve managerial discretion over the spread of hours worked, and utilise production time better. This will allow employers to tailor their labour requirements more effectively to the particular needs of their enterprise, and to respond more effectively to seasonal influences and fluctuating demand.

To a lesser extent, negotiations are also focusing on institutional rigidities in the way work is organised, particularly where they result in poor utilisation of skills and restrict people from being used in a number of different functions. Common issues raised in negotiations include manning and demarcation agreements, reviews of work classifications and restrictions on duties within the same classification. The changes involved have potential benefits not only for management, but also for employees through more variable and responsible work tasks and improved job satisfaction. Second-tier negotiations are also encompassing dispute-avoidance procedures, improved equipment utilisation and agreements on the introduction of new technology.

The relative slowness in negotiations is not unexpected in view of the fact that many of the practices in question involve long-established conditions and are frequently backed up by a strong organisational or industry culture which makes change difficult. Some managerial and union officers have had difficulty questioning their current work practices, methods of production and enterprise strategies. In addition, both sides have experienced some unfamiliarity with the new bargaining process.

In many cases, development of the necessary bargaining skills and attitudinal changes has been required. It has also been necessary to develop different bargaining arrangements suited to the requirements of different industries and enterprises.

In the building industry, for example, the transient nature of the workplace, the number of subcontractors involved on large sites, and other considerations inherent to the industry made enterprise-based negotiations unsuitable and necessitated a national agreement supplemented by agreements at the state level. In most other cases, negotiations have focused on the enterprise or company level, but in complex industries comprising numerous enterprises, such a the metal industry, a national framework has been established within which both industry-wide and decentralised negotiations could take place.

In some of the cases brought before the Arbitration Commission to date, the tribunal has commended the parties for the way they have approached their discussions, suggesting a degree of maturity in relationships which has not been present in the past. There is evidence of attitudinal as well as structural change – involving a shared awareness of the need for greater efficiency and of the relationship between an industry's viability and the security and quality of employment it can offer.

While negotiations related to restructuring and efficiency are progressing on a wide front, developments in the areas of supplementary payments and superannuation are proceeding only gradually and on a more limited basis.

3. Developments regarding employers' organisations

Since 1977, national employer representation on industrial relations and wage-fixing matters has been through the Confederation of Australian Industry (CAI) – a co-ordinating organisation representative of employers, organised at state level through umbrella associations and at national level through industry associations. Since 1983, other organisations representing specific sectors have also become involved in industrial relations matters (for example, the Business Council of Australia representing a number of major companies, and other organisations representing rural interests and small businesses). Some groups have recently argued for the abolition of the arbitration system and deregulation of industrial relations based on a system of contracts negotiated at the level of the enterprise or company.

In mid-1987 the CAI released an Employer agenda which outlines the policy direction employers believe the Government should pursue on major current industrial relations issues as well as indicating future employer strategies. The CAI considers that the second-tier arrangements have shifted a degree of control over industrial relations matters back to individual employers, and encourages employers to use the opportunity to the maximum benefit of the enterprise and to review practices at the enterprise level. The CAI has encouraged employers at the industry and national levels to take initiatives to ensure the genuine elimination of restrictive work practices.

The CAI's agenda stresses the need for education and training systems to become more responsive to the changing needs of industry, and supports employee participation in the decision-making processes of enterprises. The need for greater employer unity is envisaged, particularly if the rationalisation of union structures occurs, which will reduce the number of unions (see below). While general support is expressed for the conciliation and arbitration system, reforms are suggested, including more effective sanctions for the tribunals and, more fundamentally, maintenance of the shift in responsibility for industrial relations to the level of the individual enterprise.

4. Developments regarding workers' organisations

Following its amalgamation in the 1970s with top union bodies covering the public sector, the ACTU represents virtually all Australian unions: nearly 95 per cent of Australian unionists belong to ACTU-affiliated unions. Recent developments under the Accord have seen the ACTU's involvement in economic and industrial relations policy formulation enhanced. However, official statistics have suggested a decline in trade union membership over the past decade, from 51 per cent of the workforce in 1976 to 46 per cent in 1986 (comprising 34 per cent private sector, 71 per cent public sector). Australian unions, of which there are some 300, are organised substantially along craft lines.

There are several possible explanations for this trend, including: the restructuring of industry away from the traditionally more highly unionised manufacturing sector towards the service and finance sectors; an increase in part-time work and the rise in female participation in the workforce – both groups being associated with lower levels of union membership; and an increase in the proportion of younger employees in the workforce with a tendency not to join trade unions.

In the face of declining membership, economic deterioration and other pressures, the ACTU has developed policies outlined in *Future strategies for the union movement*. The proposed strategies include:

- rationalisation of Australia's union structure by amalgamations to form unions organised on broad industry lines, employing more people with responsibilities for direct contact with employers and offering an expanded range of services;

- industry councils involving employers and governments to be a focal point for industry discussions on general issues such as investment, technological change, employment, training and international trends;
- defending and consolidating a reformed conciliation and arbitration system; and
- maintaining and consolidating existing links between the union movement and the Australian Labour Party to enable the movement to exert a positive influence on legislative programmes and to be involved in national economic management.

The ACTU's *Future strategies* document has recently been supplemented by the report of a recent mission to Western Europe including representatives of the ACTU. The report of the mission members, entitled *Australia reconstructed*, makes a number of policy recommendations designed to address Australia's balance-of-payments problem based on consideration of the experience and policies of a number of European countries. The report advocates a consensus approach to macro-economic management involving formal and informal co-operation between the Government, unions and business with supplementary policy recommendations designed to:

- provide a stable economic environment by means of an incomes policy based on maintenance of a centralised wage-fixing system;
- support efficient industries and encourage industry restructuring and productive investment;
- develop active labour market policies focusing on skill formation, job placement and the reduction of labour market segmentation; and
- develop strategic unionism and promote industrial democracy.

Australia reconstructed received the endorsement of the 1987 ACTU Congress.

5. The role of the Government

The Australian Constitution limits the ability of the federal Government to legislate directly on industrial relations, except in the case of its own employees and territories. The Government has an important influence on the system, however, through several "indirect" means:

- first, by establishing and maintaining the legislative framework for the federal tribunal system;
- second, through strong and direct advocacy for a centralised wage-fixing system; and
- third, by developing and implementing policies supportive of the centralised wage-fixing system.

The Government is represented as an intervener in the public interest in National Wage Case proceedings, and its views are generally accorded substantial importance by the Commission. The Government has sought to implement its wages policy through the operations of the Commission. Fulfilment of the third role has involved the Government in a range of activities including the maintenance of a consultative and consensus approach to economic management and industry policy, formalised through tripartite forums such as the Economic Planning Advisory Council, National Labour Consultative Council, the Australia Manufacturing Council and various industry councils. It also ensures the co-ordination of industrial relations within its own sphere of employment so that federal public sector wages and conditions are reviewed in line with the Commission's wage principles.

Employers, however, remain critical of the degree of government intervention in industrial relations, particularly through the Accord with the ACTU.

The Government has indicated its strong support for the development of industrial democracy and employee participation in workplaces, not only because it is socially equitable, but also as an effective complement to other policies designed to enhance workplace and national productivity. It has released a policy discussion paper canvassing issues relating to industrial democracy and, in the near future, will be finalising its policy having regard to the responses received.

Consideration is also currently being given to reform of federal industrial legislation following the report of a tripartite inquiry into Australian industrial relations law and systems.

6. The climate of collective bargaining

A primary objective of the changed relationships between the Government, employers and trade unions has been to improve industrial relations to the benefit of workers, employers and the community generally through the development of a more rational and co-operative approach to industrial relations and wage determination. While it is recognised that industrial dispute statistics are only partial indicators of the state of industrial relations, they demonstrate a substantial improvement in industrial stability and evidence a more co-operative approach to the resolution of industrial conflict over the past four years. Employers, however, have been concerned about the growth of bans and limitations on work as a form of industrial action.

Since 1982-83, official statistics indicate that working days lost due to industrial disputes have fallen by some 60 per cent compared with the previous four years. The sharp contrast with past experience is significant, as industrial conflict declined at a time of marked improvement in economic activity, corporate profits and employment. Typically this combination of factors would have been expected to have led to a resurgence in industrial unrest and wage pressures. The reverse has occurred. Despite the attitudinal adjustments associated with second-tier negotiations, there has been no upsurge in industrial action under the new wage system.

These figures clearly suggest a trend towards more co-operation and less conflict in industrial relations, but further progress is required. The level of co-operation achieved will depend upon a range of factors including the continued viability of the wage system and ongoing attitudinal change at the workplace level. The experience of positive local negotiations under the second tier of the wage system may encourage the parties to become involved in similar exercises in future. An enhanced awareness of common interests and of the economic performance needs of enterprises and industries would have longer-term benefits. In addition, where second-tier negotiations result in the establishment of disputes procedures and consultative arrangements, for example relating to the introduction of new technology, the prospects of a more co-operative approach will be further enhanced.

7. Conclusion

The Australian Government considers that much has been achieved from the co-operative relationship between the Government, employers and the union movement. Industrial harmony has been enhanced while the wage system has worked to avoid the resurgence of wage inflation which has undermined previous economic recoveries in Australia. More recently, the system has adapted to meet the significant external constraints imposed on the Australian economy from abroad. Through the Arbitration Commission a system for determining wages and conditions of employment has been put into place which also has the substantial support of employers. The two-tier wage system balances the need for an equitable, but restrained approach to wage fixing with the need for industrial restructuring and workplace reform and achieves this through an arrangement combining more decentralised bargaining within a centrally determined framework.

The two-tier system is to operate until mid-1988 when it is to be reviewed. At this time, the Government, employer groups and unions are giving consideration as to how the system may be revised. The Government sees merit in the retention of efficiency and productivity improvements as an important basis for future wage increases. While maintaining avenues for equity considerations to be further pursued, the Government believes that any revised wage system must also build on the contribution being made by the current system towards desirable structural change in the economy. The wage system can play a significant role in complementing wider industry and enterprise development strategies with the restructuring of awards to encourage skill formation and greater flexibility of operation. There is growing tripartite support in Australia for such objectives, which augurs well for the achievement of a stronger consensus base underpinning the evolution of wage-fixing arrangements in Australia.

Collective bargaining in Austria: Recent trends and problems

The Federal Ministry of Labour and Social Affairs, in co-operation with the Austrian Congress of Chambers of Workers, the Federal Economic Chamber, the Confederation of Austrian Trade Unions, the Association of Austrian Industrialists

1. Economic background to collective bargaining

Economic conditions have changed considerably in Austria since the last Symposium on Collective Bargaining, held in November 1977 and – apart from inflation and the balance of trade – the changes have been very much for the worse. Real economic growth of 4.7 per cent was recorded in 1979, while in the first half of the 1980s it fell to a meagre average of 1.6 per cent a year. It was not much higher in 1986 at 1.8 per cent; the forecast for 1987 was below 1 per cent. Apart from recent cyclical problems caused primarily by the weakness of the United States dollar and reduced demand from oil-producing countries, structural adjustment problems have also played an important role. The steel industry, mostly nationalised, is in the middle of a modernisation and rationalisation process which has brought considerable social and regional difficulties in its wake.

As a result of weak economic growth in recent years, the unemployment rate has also risen. It was as low as 2 per cent in 1980; after the collapse of the labour market in 1981-82 it rose to 3.7 per cent and reached 5.2 per cent in 1986. It was estimated that unemployment would continue to be below 6 per cent in 1987 but medium-term forecasts predicted an increase of 0.25 to 0.5 per cent per annum far into the 1990s. This development has mainly demographic causes and affects young people more than others. This can be seen from the fact that, despite growing unemployment since 1983, the number of people in work has increased. There were about 45,000 more employed people in 1986 than in 1983. It appears that labour market developments in the next few years will continue in the direction of higher unemployment, due to the belated baby boom in Austria. In other industrial countries this phenomenon has now largely run its course (in the European OECD countries, unemployment rates have been constant, on average, for about three years).

The trend towards increased employment in services continues, though growth is slowing down. At present, about 55 per cent of wage earners are employed in the service sector. This has also resulted in a shift within the labour market between men and women: since 1983 the unemployment rate has been higher among men than among women, whereas the unemployment rate for women was almost twice as high as that for men in 1977.

Contract staff pose little problem in Austria; their potential share of the labour market is estimated at about 2.5 per cent. None the less, serious endeavours are under way to resolve by a special Act the questions of labour and social rights for contract

Table 1. Trade union membership, 1976-86

	Membership, 1986	Change, 1976-86 (%)
Total OGB[1]	1 670	+1.2
Clerical staff	348	+12.9
Public service	226	+33.1
Municipal staff	169	+11.4
Art and media	18	+16.3
Construction, timber	184	-2.4
Chemicals	58	-13.6
Railways	117	-0.7
Printing, paper	24	-3.0
Commerce, transport	38	+21.7
Catering, personal service	52	+24.1
Agriculture, forestry	19	-15.5
Foodstuffs	43	-6.6
Metalwork, mining, power	251	-10.9
Textiles, clothing, leather	47	-31.3
Postal service	77	+14.2
	1976 (%)	1986 (%)
Union organisation rate	59.6	60.0
As proportion of union members:		
Women	30	31 (approx.)
Clerical staff, etc.	51.8	57.2

[1] Confederation of Austrian Trade Unions.

staff. "Atypical" jobs (for example, employment on social projects) have had to be substantially curtailed, primarily for financial reasons, but also because their meaningfulness has frequently been cast into doubt. An unchanging and serious problem is illicit work, which accounts for an estimated 7 to 10 per cent of gross national product.

Except for minor fluctuations, the number of trade union members and the degree of unionisation among workers have remained broadly constant over the last ten years. The detailed figures for 1986 are given in table 1 for the OGB (Confederation of Austrian Trade Unions) and for its member unions, along with the percentage change from 1976.

The table also sets out the main changes in the structure of organised labour. The percentage of white-collar employees, civil servants (including the post office and the railways) and people employed in institutions of art and culture and in the media rose from 51 per cent of total trade union membership in 1976 to 57.2 per cent in 1986. This means that blue-collar worker membership in unions has dropped from more than 48 per cent in 1976 to less than 43 per cent in 1986.

The relative and absolute increase in the number of white-collar union members means that heterogeneous groups – in the fields of art and media, social services, national administration, qualified technical and commercial professions – which are not closely connected to the traditions of trade union policy, have greater weight within the union movement than before. This, together with higher unemployment and a decline in traditional leading industries has challenged labour representatives, including the statutory representative bodies and the Workers' Chambers to establish their authority. The traditional bargaining methods used by labour representatives, including the mechanics of the social partnership, are frequently criticised as inadequate and over-hierarchical without, however, there being any promising alternative options available.

The trade unions are attempting to solve these problems, as well as the loss of members in the mining, metalworking, chemical and textile industries. On the one hand, attempts have been made to involve members directly in the decision-making process to a greater extent and, on the other hand, to recruit new members in expanding sectors. Open-minded and active treatment of pressing issues related to future developments, such as co-determination of working conditions for the introduction and expansion of new technologies as well as training policy, should help workers to cope with the structural adjustment process within the trade union movement.

Basic changes in the organisational structure of trade unions, for instance, grouping workers by industry instead of the separate representation of white-collar workers, as at present, is occasionally suggested in inter-union discussions but is not a realistic prospect in the immediate future. Closer collaboration between unions beyond the confines of the individual organisations, and greater assistance for workers in small and medium-sized enterprises in line with structural changes are, however, prime goals.

The splitting up of a firm into sections, the award of certain jobs within the enterprise to outside companies and the use of contract labour pose considerable problems for the effective representation of labour. Legal regulations for these new forms of labour would appear essential to prevent further inequalities in protection under the labour and social laws, including the opportunity for unions to represent such workers.

Collective bargaining by employers is conducted primarily by the Chambers of Commerce and their divisions. Membership of the Chambers is compulsory. Accordingly, at a superficial glance, there does not seem to be a membership recruitment problem. A careful analysis, however, shows that on the employers' side too, members have doubts as to the efficiency of their associations. The area of discussion, over pay and over social laws, is thus continually reduced. On the other hand, the need for harmony and agreement is clearly recognised. The position may best be characterised by saying that a "limited conflict" with the unions would possibly be welcome, provided it could be kept within bounds. Warnings of such conflicts from the employers' associations are however deemed a sign of weakness. A special problem on the employers' side is posed by the steel industry, as collective agreements have to apply both to the nationalised industry with its heavy financial deficit, and to the private sector. Increases in actual wages and salaries, customary in industry for decades, are also meeting growing resistance from employers.

2. The role of the State in labour relations

The Austrian system of social partnership enshrined in the Paritätischen Kommission (Joint Committee) on price and wage problems involves tripartite co-operation between the Government and representatives of employers and workers. However, the Committee's scope is largely confined to the discussion of economic and social principles. Co-operation is demonstrated chiefly in the periodic discussions about economic policy between the Government and the social partners, to which certain experts, for example, the President of the Austrian National Bank, economic researchers, etc. are invited.

The Government does not directly influence the results of collective bargaining through this kind of social partnership. The arrangement whereby the organisation wishing to reopen a collective bargaining so informs the Joint Committee, whose Subcommittee on Wages sanctions negotiations, is merely a self-imposed control by the social partners. Such decisions have to be reached by consensus and without government participation.

This system has been maintained despite increasing economic difficulties. It should also be mentioned in this connection that it is many years since bargaining proposals were met by intervention from the Wages Subcommittee.

The International Labour Office has suggested that Austria's social partnership system has run into problems in recent years. This criticism may stem from Austria's less favourable economic performance than in the past. In addition, the social partnership has been criticised on rather theoretical grounds by mainly academic groups which are concerned with its role within society and in determining legislation. This criticism is in part directed at the extent of influence exerted by the social partnership which reaches far beyond matters of collective bargaining, without adequate democratic authority. In as far as social partnership agreements lead to subsequent enactment of laws, they involve – in the opinion of some critics – a curtailment of parliamentary institutions because the parties forming the Government feel bound by them. Equally, the social partnership's ability to solve pending problems of an economic or social policy nature is increasingly called into question. Such criticism, however, can be countered by contrary examples from the recent past. For instance, in 1986 lengthy discussions between the social partners resulted in a consensus on new legal provisions to further the development of co-determination as demanded by the trade unions for many years.

3. The structure of collective bargaining

Little change has taken place in the system of decentralised collective bargaining in Austria. About 500 agreements are concluded in each wage round. The procedures of both parties are, to a large extent, bound by tradition. Decentralised bargaining by trade and region is characteristic in small-scale industry, whereas a higher degree of centralisation is found in the major industries. Here, industry-wide agreements are usually concluded for the whole country.

A major development has taken place since 1985 in negotiations on the reduction and reorganisation of working time. Previously, reductions of working time had been negotiated centrally between the Federal Chamber of Commerce and the Confederation of Austrian Trade Unions in the form of global collective agreements. Since 1985 this has been subject to negotiation at the level of trade association and specific unions. From the viewpoint of the employers' organisations, this development is seen as positive because it enables the circumstances of individual industries to be taken into account. On the other hand, doubts are occasionally voiced on the employees' side, as this development could conflict with the solidarity of wages policy. The differences in social rights have certainly widened as a result of decentralised collective bargaining. The decentralisation process will probably continue, as it is becoming increasingly difficult for both sides to enforce uniform solutions among their members.

Collective agreements by individual companies still play an important role in Austria. It is not planned to expand them, nor does that seem likely.

With the growing decentralisation of working time negotiations, certain problems naturally occur in co-ordination. However, these are manageable because the organisations are highly decentralised. Moreover developments at the level of trade associations are so varied that the agreements reached can be decreasingly used as a pattern for other industries.

Problems crop up in co-ordination between the public and private sectors. Agreements reached for the economy as a whole are not only applied in the protected field of public services, but are even exceeded, although budget constraints should warrant extreme thriftiness there.

4. The content of collective bargaining

Each year more than 500 collective agreements are concluded on the basis of negotiations between the social partners and these are generally applicable to an entire industry for the federal provinces or for the whole federal territory (the figure was 538 such agreements in 1985 and 587 in 1986).

The main content of the collective agreements remains the fixing of minimum wages, of bonuses and allowances for certain jobs, and the setting-up of principles for piece-work systems.

In the last two years a reduction of standard working hours has been included in collective agreements in order to create new jobs or avoid job losses. (The individual industries where this has happened – up to the summer of 1987 – are listed in table 2.)

It is to be assumed that the reduction of working time will be a focus of union attention in the near future, in order to obtain uniform arrangements across industry as a whole. The objective would be to extend the application of shorter working time in Austria, and to prevent divergences in labour and social rights in different sectors of the economy, which would adversely affect the overall structure of working conditions in the country.

Table 2. Industries implementing a reduction of weekly working hours

Industry[1]	Average normal weekly hours
Graphic industry	38
Crude-oil industry	38
Iron and metalworking	38.5
Power supply	38.5
Mining	38.5
Salt mining	38
Crude-oil trading	38
Edible oils and fats	38.5
Newspapers	38
Grain milling	38
Confectionery	38.5
Fruit and vegetable processing, deep freeze industry	38.5
Dairies	38.5
Paper manufacture	38
Paper and board processing trades	38
Chemical industry	38.5
Tobacco trade	38.5
Private insurance, office services	38.5

[1] Comprising in total more than 550,000 employed persons (about 20 per cent of all employees).

The modest but solidaristic wages policy pursued by many unions in recent years has to be seen in the context of pressures for work flexibility and the prevention of job losses through excessive cost increases for employers. Wage policy has been modest in the sense that, especially in industries affected by crises, wage demands have not always included productivity growth, and in some years increases have been below the rate of inflation. Wage policy has been solidaristic in demanding a narrowing of wage differentials (for instance, through increases of a fixed amount or the award of higher-percentage increases to low-paid workers).

This policy, as well as increasing unemployment, contributed to the drop in the adjustment wage quota from 72.9 per cent in 1976 to 68.7 per cent in 1985, when it was back to the level of 1970. Wage earners have had only minor increases in real income since 1976. Since wages provide mass-purchasing power, this development poses problems and cannot continue without limit especially given the pressure on the unions to exert their authority.

Collective agreements relating in particular to the effects of technological progress on jobs and working conditions have been negotiated by the unions for the first time in recent years. Special mention should be made of a collective agreement for the printing industry and the media, which covered temporary arrangements to deal with transitional problems caused by the introduction of film composition. These included job protection for employees, retraining and additional severance pay for redundant workers.

Of late, the unions have also tried to tackle problems arising from the hiving-off of activities within an enterprise (awarding specific jobs to independent contractors, or splitting up the firm). In the graphic industry, for instance, the collective agreement stipulates that contract staff are generally not permitted.

Such arrangements of a mainly obligatory nature between the contracting partners, which are a reaction to the changing structure of the economy, will assuredly gain emphasis in union bargaining policy as the trend towards hiving-off continues.

5. The climate of collective bargaining

The system of social partnership, practised in Austria for decades, has maintained the ability of employers and trade unions to communicate and solve problems despite deteriorating economic conditions. There have been few strikes in recent years, and the use of lock-outs is unknown. However, it is becoming increasingly difficult to convince members on both sides of the value of sustaining a good climate for communication between the social partners. Their representative organisations neither can nor want to dodge the need for overall political responsibility. Reducing the budget deficit, considered the Government's unalterable priority, presents greater problems for employees' representatives than employers, because of the negative effect it could have on employment levels.

New forms of closer co-operation are not being developed, probably because the system of social partnership permeates down to individual enterprises. Participation by employees is still little developed in Austria, for reasons of tax and lack of incentives.

Such systems of participation, as well as new models of labour organisation (quality circles, greater autonomy and responsibility for work groups) are, due to present labour laws, easier to set up at enterprise level between shop stewards and management than on the basis of industry-wide collective agreements. Whether or not general rules for these developments can be worked out on a legal basis or on the basis of collective agreements for whole industries will be shown by experience of using these new types of labour organisation.

Fears that the unions might lose influence due to new forms of co-operation have not been confirmed in practice. The unions and their shop stewards have generally managed to safeguard their position. Whether or not there is a strategy on the employers' side to weaken the influence of the unions or the workers' representatives within the enterprise, by means of staff participation and new job forms, cannot be determined at this time from the facts.

In conclusion, it appears that economic difficulties and increasing unemployment can, on the one hand, strengthen the inclination of social partners to take joint steps to overcome problems (for instance, by the reduction of working time), but on the other hand may weaken their chances of reaching agreement in certain cases because of higher expectations of the membership. The possibilities of failure to agree, and thus labour disputes following unsuccessful collective bargaining, could increase in future. In 1986, such conflicts were staved off (in some areas) only with considerable difficulty.

Collective bargaining in Ontario, Canada: Recent trends and problems (from 1973 to the present)

Mr. Victor Pathe, Assistant Deputy-Minister, Industrial Relations Division, Ministry of Labour of Ontario

1. Introduction

This paper looks at some of the general issues and patterns which have emerged over the last 15 years in Ontario's collective bargaining system. A description of the Ontario economy and its collective bargaining framework is followed by an examination of how the collective bargaining system has responded to the tumultuous period since 1973. The paper concludes with a section on how collective bargaining in 1987 differed from the era prior to 1973 and another on the future of the collective bargaining system.

(a) The Ontario economy

Canada is a federal State in which legislative powers are divided between the national and provincial governments. In the domain of labour relations most of the law-making powers reside at the provincial level. The federal Government is responsible for a limited number of industries that constitute approximately 10 per cent of the workforce: e.g. inter-provincial transportation (air, rail and road), radio and television facilities, banking and employees of the national Government and its agencies. The remaining 90 per cent of employees are covered by labour legislation enacted at the provincial level. This includes nearly all employees working in the private sector along with those in such public sector areas as education, hospitals, municipalities and employees of the provincial government.

Ontario is Canada's most industrialised province, accounting for about 37 per cent of the country's gross domestic product and generating 39 per cent of the jobs. Much of the province's economic strength derives from its manufacturing sector. Forty-seven per cent of the country's manufacturing jobs are located in Ontario and 52 per cent of the nation's manufacturing GDP comes from this province. Most of the manufacturing activity is located in the southern part of the province where there is ready access to American markets located around the Great Lakes. The northern part of the province is more sparsely populated and its economy is based largely on natural resources, i.e. mining and forestry.

Since the Second World War the structure of employment has been gradually shifting away from manufacturing and towards the service sector. In 1951, 32 per cent of the jobs in Ontario were in manufacturing and 14 per cent were in the service sector. By 1985 there had been a considerable reversal. The service sector now constitutes about 31 per cent of the workforce, while manufacturing has dropped to 23 per cent.

The most important segment of Ontario's manufacturing sector is automobile production. Nearly all the country's production facilities are located in southern Ontario (namely Chrysler, Ford and General Motors) and new facilities being built by Japanese investors (Honda, Toyota and Suzuki) have either just come into production or will in the next year or so. But, while automobiles are the most significant part of Ontario's manufacturing sector, a wide array of other kinds of manufacturing facility is also to be found in the province.

(b) The Ontario economy since the Second World War

Ontario's experience over the last 35 years has been not unlike that of other industrialised economies. Until the early 1970s the province enjoyed a post-war boom that was characterised by sustained growth, low unemployment rates and low rates of inflation. Between 1951 and 1970, the average rate of unemployment in the province was 3.6 per cent of the labour force. Prices rose, on average, by 2.2 per cent per annum during the 1950s, and by 2.9 per cent in the 1960s (see table 1).

However, between 1973 and 1986 the rate of unemployment in Ontario nearly doubled to an average of 7.1 per cent; the average annual increase in consumer prices was 8.1 per cent during this time; and economic growth averaged a disappointing 2.7 per cent. Ontario's collective bargaining system, as in the rest of the industrialised world, has had to cope with these adverse circumstances. Over the last few years,

Table 1. Unemployment rates and consumer price indexes, 1951-86

	Ontario unemployment rate (Average annual rate in percentages)	Consumer price index, Canada (Average annual increase in percentages)
1951-60	3.6	2.2
1961-70	3.6	2.9
1973-86	7.1	8.1
1973	4.3	7.7
1974	4.4	10.9
1975	6.3	10.8
1976	6.2	7.5
1977	7.0	7.9
1978	7.2	8.8
1979	6.5	9.2
1980	6.8	10.2
1981	6.6	12.5
1982	9.8	10.8
1983	10.4	5.8
1984	9.1	4.4
1985	8.0	4.0
1986	7.0	4.2

however, Ontario, in contrast with most of the remainder of Canada, has been experiencing a relatively strong economic recovery.

Although data for Ontario *per se* do not exist, it can be inferred that the rate of growth in manufacturing productivity has been rather dismal since 1973. The national data indicate that between 1973 and 1985 Canada had the lowest rate of increase in manufacturing productivity (averaging 1.9 per cent per annum) of 12 major industrial countries. Since roughly half of Canada's manufacturing is located in Ontario, it seems safe to conclude that the province's overall productivity performance has been uninspiring. One factor that has helped to maintain the competitive position of Canadian manufacturers against their main trading rivals (in the United States) has been the decline of the Canadian dollar vis-à-vis the American since the mid-1970s.

(c) The framework of collective bargaining in Ontario

Readers familiar with the United States will recognise a number of similarities between that country's collective bargaining framework and Ontario's. In both jurisdictions collective bargaining tends to take place at a decentralised level. This is in good part due to the process by which unions obtain the right to represent workers. Unions generally obtain representation rights for a particular workplace (provided it is demonstrated that the union is wanted by a majority of the workers). The representation rights for the workplace become the bargaining rights; the legislation requires the employer to bargain with that union and most resulting collective agreements apply to one employer and one union.

If the negotiations between a union and employer do not result in a settlement, then the union or employer can engage in a work stoppage. However, it has been found that in Ontario 96 to 97 per cent of negotiations reach a settlement without resorting to a work stoppage. (In some public sector negotiations – hospital employees, police, fire-fighters and provincial civil servants – work stoppages are prohibited; for those employees an impasse is resolved through binding arbitration.)

In some industries more centralised bargaining structures evolved over successive rounds of negotiations. In some industries, such as construction, this took the form of multi-employer bargaining; in others, such as automobile manufacturing and the pulp and paper industry, it was multi-plant. How some of these more centralised structures fared over the last decade will be mentioned later.

While much of the foregoing shows the Ontario labour relations system to resemble the American one, there is one area in which their experiences have differed over the last decade. It is well-known that the degree of unionisation in the United States has been steadily declining to the point that now less than 20 per cent of the American workforce is unionised. Contrary to that, the proportion of the workforce that is unionised in Ontario has remained fairly constant at about 33 per cent. This may in part be explained by the expansion of unionisation in Ontario's public sector over the last 15 years.

2. Collective bargaining from 1973 to 1986

While the collective bargaining system in Ontario was operating in difficult circumstances throughout the 1973 to 1986 period, the underlying factors were shifting. Five separate subperiods can be identified in which the collective bargaining system was required to react to different sets of factors and economic conditions.

(a) 1973 to 1975 (third quarter)

The first oil-price shock in 1973 led to inflation becoming much more rampant in Ontario. In the early 1970s, inflation had been running at about 3 per cent. But the rate rose to 7.7 per cent in 1973, reached 10.9 per cent in 1974, and in 1975 remained at 10.8 per cent. This had the disturbing effect of seriously eroding negotiated wage increases.

Unions attempted to protect real wages by doing the following: (1) where parties were in a multi-year agreement that had been negotiated before the onset of more rapid inflation, unions asked employers to reopen the agreement voluntarily (the unions have no means by which to force the reopening of an agreement before its expiry date). A number of employers (but by no means a majority) voluntarily made mid-contract wage adjustments to take into account the rate of inflation. (2) When collective agreements expired, unions successfully negotiated better inflation protection either by getting cost-of-living allowance (COLA) clauses or very high wage increases (and occasionally getting both). COLA clauses were seen as the price an employer had to pay in order to get a multi-year collective agreement. In 1974, negotiated wage increases (in agreements without COLAs) averaged 13.4 per cent per annum, and in 1975 the average rose to 15.3 per cent. Thus, unionised employees were keeping ahead of the rapid rate of inflation, but this made the collective bargaining system look as though it was contributing to a volatile and unstable situation. It reinforced a pattern that has continued to this day, which is that the struggle between unions and employers over the distribution of income has produced a form of labour relations lacking the co-operative and accommodative features that some other countries have developed.

(b) 1975 (fourth quarter) to 1978 (first quarter)

The federal Government became so concerned about the wage-price spiral that it invoked controls in October 1975. The programme applied to both wage and price increases, and was originally to last for three years, but was phased out after 30 months. The general wage increases allowed under the controls programme were 10 per cent in the first year (i.e. after their current collective agreement expired), 8 per cent in the second year, and 6 per cent in the third.

The labour movement was unhappy with the programme because it perceived the controls as unfairly clamping down on wages more than on prices. At the start of the programme there were predictions of an increase in the level of labour-management confrontation (i.e. strikes and lock-outs), but in fact the level of work stoppages was somewhat reduced during this period. The reason for this had less to do with eventual trade union acceptance of the controls and more with the futility of engaging in economic actions to oppose them.

In the first year of the controls, the rate of inflation dropped by over 3 per cent (down from 10.8 per cent to 7.5 per cent) and by the second year average wage settlements were no longer around in the 12 to 15 per cent range, but had fallen to 7.9 per cent. In the final year of the controls, wage settlements were still being brought down (to 6.8 per cent in 1978) while inflation had started to rise again, reaching 12.5 per cent by 1981.

One other factor came into play at this time. The Canadian dollar began to fall in terms of the American dollar and this continued for about a decade, leaving wage costs in Canada more competitive than they would otherwise have been. But while the combined effects of the controls and the devaluation of the dollar made it possible to combat inflation without generating even more unemployment (as would have been the case had the federal Government chosen to fight inflation by deflating the economy), the labour movement saw its standing diminished in the economic community.

(c) 1978 (second quarter) to 1982 (third quarter)

In 1976 the Canadian dollar stood at US$1.01. Over the next ten years the Canadian dollar fell an average of 3.7 per cent a year and by 1985 was worth roughly US$0.73. This provided some room for wage increases to start creeping up again after the controls programme had ended, even though the economy was not performing all that well.

In this period the phrase "stagflation" entered the language. As with other industrialised economies, Ontario's growth was stagnant while inflation was not abating. Between 1978 and 1981 economic growth was a mere 1.5 per cent per year; at the same time inflation was rising by 10.6 per cent annually. Negotiated wage increases were keeping up with the pace of inflation, averaging 10.2 per cent during that period. This was brought to a halt with the recession in the early 1980s.

(d) 1982 (fourth quarter) to 1983 (fourth quarter)

The severe world-wide economic downturn experienced by most of the industrial economies in the early 1980s was felt in Ontario during 1982 and 1983. The province's economy shrank by 4.1 per cent in 1982 and growth in 1983 only brought the level of economic activity back to where it had been in 1981. The unemployment rate in Ontario rose to 9.8 per cent in 1982 and the following year it hit a post-war high of 10.4 per cent.

In response to the downturn, the federal Government applied wage controls to its public sector in the middle of 1982 and in September the Ontario government did likewise to public sector employees in its jurisdiction. The provincial programme overrode the wage adjustments scheduled in existing collective agreements and mandated the increases by 5 per cent per annum over a two-year period. Just prior to this controls programme, wage increases in the Ontario public sector had been running at 11 to 12 per cent per annum.

Negotiated settlements in Ontario's private sector were not very far behind the size of public sector increases in the summer of 1982. But 18 months later the effect of the economic downturn had caused negotiated wage settlements in the private sector to fall precipitately to 4 per cent on average.

During the downturn in 1982, unionists had become concerned that what they were observing in American bargaining – for example, wage freezes, wage give-backs, two-tiered wage rates, etc. – would spread to Canada. The Canadian labour movement vowed to resist "concession bargaining". The unions in Ontario were generally more successful at resisting concessions, although their gains were small compared to previous periods. A trend was emerging in which unions were able on average to achieve wage increases equal to the rate of inflation, i.e. real wages were tending more or less to stand still. This contrasts with much of the previous post-war period when wage increases on average exceeded the rate of inflation by a couple of percentage points (roughly equivalent to the rate of improvement in productivity).

The recession forced employers to focus more than ever on their competitiveness. Not only were direct wage costs a consideration, but employers also sought greater flexibility in their operations (in connection with work rules, job classifications, etc.). On the opposite side, workers came to view job security with greater importance.

Finally, the economic downturn was partly responsible for the disintegration of some of the more centralised forms of bargaining that had developed over the years. The recession did not have the same impact on all employers; those hit hard by it lost their interest in being part of a bargaining structure that included employers not suffering to the same degree. The result was to return to bargaining at a more local level in some industries.

(e) From 1984 to the present

Since 1984, Ontario has been experiencing a rather strong recovery, concentrated primarily in the southern part of the province. The northern part of the province has been recovering more slowly because its resource industries have been more sluggish than the south's manufacturing.

The rate of inflation has been relatively stable at about 4 per cent, though there are recent signs that it is on the increase in the prosperous areas of southern Ontario. There has been a continuation of the trend for negotiable wage increases merely to keep pace with the inflation rate while unions stress job security at the bargaining table. Competitiveness remains a concern for employers.

3. How collective bargaining in 1987 differs from the years prior to 1973

In the 1950s and 1960s the collective bargaining system concentrated on distributing the growing economic abundance. Unions could go for real wage gains without much fear of adverse employment effects; and employers could pass along the costs of these gains to the consumer. With regard to technological change and industrial restructuring, there seemed to be fewer employee displacement problems because the buoyant economy made absorption of affected workers less difficult. In retrospect, that period looks like something of a golden age for the collective bargaining system.

In contrast, the current economic situation has been putting greater strains on the bargaining system and has produced an atmosphere which is considerably less optimistic. Unions have become more concerned with protecting the job security of their members. Also, bargaining for improved pensions and early retirement schemes has become one of the more frequent union objectives. Where reductions in manpower requirements are unavoidable, the best the union can do is to protect the future standard of living of those who retire. We have recently seen the situation in automobile negotiations where the younger members of the bargaining unit favour negotiating early retirement improvements because, if the older workers are enticed to retire, the fewer jobs that remain can be distributed among the younger workers.

The preoccupation with job security has manifested itself in other areas as well. Unions are showing more interest, for example, in limiting the degree to which employers contract out work that could be performed by their members.

If the unions are more concerned with job security, it is in part because of the employers' increasing drive for greater competitiveness. Where international trade is a relatively small factor in the degree of competition being faced, an employer's domestic competitors may be facing the same wage costs, particularly in industries in which unions have successfully organised most or all of the major companies. In the 1950s and 1960s, the bargaining parties in Ontario were afforded a certain latitude in their bargaining because wages had to some degree been taken out of competition. (This did not prevail, though, to the same extent as it did in the United States in that period, since international trade was always a more important factor in the Ontario economy.) However, international trade has become an even more important factor than it was 15 years ago. Between 1971 and 1983, exports as a proportion of Ontario's gross domestic product grew from 20.3 per cent to 27.5 per cent; and over the same period imports rose from 22 per cent of GDP in 1971 to 30.1 per cent in 1983. As a result, the bargaining parties in Ontario can no longer be as oblivious to their competitors in other industrialised economies.

The quest for competitiveness has meant that employers are now putting on the bargaining table more of their own demands, which are receiving more serious consideration than would have been the case 15 or 20 years ago. One of the more common demands is for greater flexibility in deploying workers to various tasks. With the spread of American branch plant operations in the province over the last 50 years, Taylorism[1] was widely adopted. But now it is the Japanese production methods that are getting attention from some of the major employers in the province. The degree to which the Japanese will be emulated in Ontario, though, is still an unanswered question.

The changing composition of the Ontario workforce has also altered the collective bargaining picture over the last 15 years. As was mentioned, the relative size of the manufacturing sector has been gradually declining. This sector was the

---

[1] After Frederick Taylor, the founder of "scientific management", and his method by which jobs were divided into component tasks.

bedrock on which the trade union movement in Ontario was built. The reason this has not caused a decline in the proportion of the workforce that is unionised is due in good part to the growth of membership in the previously unorganised public sector. If the service sector continues to expand more rapidly than the others and unions do not become more successful in organising service employees, the proportion of the workforce unionised in Ontario is eventually bound to fall.

4. The future

The economic circumstances determine largely how well the collective bargaining process can deliver satisfying results. This is not to say that in adverse economic conditions the collective bargaining system will fail; it is in that situation when it can function most usefully. The following seems to be the lesson of the last 30 years: *When the economy is advancing, technological change can be introduced without too many displacement problems, which in turn means that the improvements in productivity can be passed along to the workers via the collective bargaining process. When the economic conditions are not very buoyant (because of sluggish domestic growth and/or with increased international competitiveness), the collective bargaining process becomes a defensive weapon for employees to protect themselves from displacement problems and it is not easy for the bargaining process to produce real gains.*

Over the next few years it would be expected that the collective bargaining system will continue to function in less buoyant circumstances. Despite Ontario's economic recovery, one does not sense that collective bargaining has returned to its more optimistic days. There is a lingering fear that we may not have escaped from the difficult economic times and that this is still a period of retrenchment. As long as the industrialised countries remain more concerned with recurring inflation than with reflating their economies, collective bargaining is likely to continue to function in a less buoyant situation.

Finally, at the beginning of October 1987 Canada and the United States negotiated a tentative agreement that would reduce trade barriers between the two countries. If that agreement is ratified by both Governments it could have an impact on the nature of collective bargaining. As far as Ontario is concerned the central question could become: "Do firms which now have production facilities in the province keep them in operation or do the firms supply Canadian markets from American facilities?" If the latter is the answer, then it is feared that there will be job losses and large-scale industrial restructuring. Factors affecting where firms decide to locate will be related to the relative costs of production; and wage costs will be one of these factors. As a result one could expect this to be translated into new pressures on the collective bargaining system.

Collective bargaining in Denmark: Recent trends and problems

Mr. Henrik Marstrand Dahl, Head of Division, Danish Employers' Confederation, Copenhagen

Mr. Einar Edelberg, Head of Division, Ministry of Labour of Denmark, Copenhagen

Mr. Poul Jorning, Head of Division, Danish Federation of Public Servants' and Salaried Employees' Organisations, Copenhagen

Ms. Elise Hammer Kristensen, Head of Section, Ministry of Labour of Denmark, Copenhagen

Mr. Knud Mols Sorensen, Vice-President, Salaried Employees' and Civil Servants' Federation (FTF-DK), Copenhagen

1. The context

In Denmark pay and working conditions are regulated by collective agreements both in the private and the public sectors. Widespread unionisation in the private sector at the end of the last century and other historical developments led employer and worker organisations to fight for, and win, a standard-setting function, and thus exclusivity in this field in relation to the legislature. An important element was the establishment of the distinction between disputes of rights and disputes of interests, which is still a fundamental principal of Danish labour law. This means, among other things, that disputes arising in connection with the conclusion or renewal of collective agreements may lead to work stoppages.

In addition to collective agreements there is a comprehensive system of legislation relating to labour market conditions in the broadest sense. Some of the oldest elements in the legislation are the rules concerning unemployment insurance which offer a comparatively high degree – by international standards – of unemployment compensation. Legislation has proliferated over the past 20 years or so. Some of the rules originate directly from decisions made within the European Communities, which have been incorporated in Danish legislation.

Danish labour market legislation came into existence partly in co-operation with the social partners and, in some cases, has taken the form of framework legislation where the social partners have a say in laying down the more detailed rules.

On regulation of pay and working conditions, the private sector has traditionally set the standards so that the conditions agreed on have to some extent been transferred to the public sector. This standard-setting function is, among other things, reflected in the fact that collective agreements in the private sector expire on 1 March while agreements in the public sector expire on 1 April of the same year.

(In most areas collective agreements do not contain provisions concerning job security in the form of a guarantee against dismissal or a very long dismissal notice period. The explanation is the Danish unemployment insurance system mentioned above.)

Many radical changes have taken place in the Danish labour market over recent decades. The labour force grew by about 30 per cent in the period from 1960 to 1985 and there have also been major changes in employment within the different occupational groups.

Agriculture's share of employment has shown a significant fall. Crafts and industry have also experienced a decline, while the biggest increase in employment has taken place in administration, services, and so on, and primarily in the public sector.

The Danish labour market is characterised by a very high activity rate as measured by the number of people in the labour force as a percentage of the total population in the age group 15-74 years. In 1985, 78 per cent of men were economically active, and 65 per cent of women. Twenty-five years ago the figures were 84 per cent for men and 34 per cent for women.

Furthermore, Denmark has a big public sector. In 1985 about 900,000 people were employed in the public sector, corresponding to 33 per cent of the labour force. In 1960 the public sector accounted for only 11 per cent of the labour force.

The annual increase in the wages of manual workers from 1965 until the start of the first oil crisis was about 10-12 per cent and somewhat lower for salaried employees. After three years of high wage increases in 1973, 1974 and 1975, wage rises up to 1982 rank at about 10 per cent a year, falling to about 4-5 per cent a year between 1983 and 1987. In 1987 wages were expected to rise by about 7 per cent.

Looking at trends in real disposable earnings, and taking income taxes into account, it is seen that the tax burden has been on the increase for the last ten years or so, corresponding to a drop in the real disposable income of an "average family".

2. The repercussions of economic, technological and social developments on workers' and employers' organisations

Workers' organisations

It is a characteristic feature of the Danish labour market that there is a very high degree of union membership and a highly concentrated power structure. The three central organisations are: the Federation of Danish Trade Unions (LO), the Danish Federation of Public Servants' and Salaried Employees' Organisations (FTF), and the Central Organisation of Academic Staff (AC).

In a number of areas there is close co-operation between the central organisations. Thus there are no disruptive tensions between them. Each organises distinct groups of employees.

The biggest of the central organisations is the Federation of Danish Trade Unions, which accounts for about 1.4 million employees out of a total 2 million organised employees. The Danish Federation of Public Servants' and Salaried Employees' Organisations mainly organises salaried employees in the higher-income brackets in both the public sector and the service sector. Membership is about 250,000.

Finally, there is the Central Organisation of Academic Staff for those with academic degrees, in both the private and the public sector. The total membership is a little over 75,000. There are also a number of small professional organisations which cover supervisors, salaried employees, and on so, who have an intermediate level of education.

Over the past decade the share of organised employees has gone up from 74 to 86 per cent, according to the latest survey of living conditions in Denmark. The share for men has risen from 81 to 89 per cent and that for women from 65 to 84 per cent.

Female salaried employees in the highest social category employed in the public sector are the best organised group in Denmark, with a rate of 98 per cent. This illustrates that organisation rates tend to increase the higher a person is on the social scale.

Public employees have a higher organisation rate than those in private employment and the lowest rates are found among the unskilled workers, in particular women, but also among salaried employees at the lowest levels with limited or no vocational skills.

As mentioned above, the Federation of Danish Trade Unions is the biggest organisation in the Danish labour market. It is not just an organisation of manual workers. About 400,000 public servants and salaried employees are members of a special union affiliated to the Federation. Thus the Federation of Danish Trade Unions is interested in safeguarding not only the interests of manual workers, but also those of salaried employees and public servants. The Federation's interest in the public sector has increased significantly throughout the 1970s and 1980s. But traditionally the Danish Federation of Public Servants' and Salaried Employees' Organisations has strongly asserted itself as the organisation for public salaried employees and public servants. Organisations in the private sector are also affiliated. This applies, for instance, to the financial sector and to high-grade salaried employees in shipping.

Public servants in the central Government belong to four central organisations which have formed a negotiating body – the TFU. In the local government sector the employee organisations have a similar body, called the KTO.

On the employee side there is close co-ordination between the TFU and the KTO. One problem for central government employees has been that the public servants' organisations negotiate earlier than contract employees, because the result of this negotiation then applies more or less unchanged to the latter who want to be represented at the negotiating table; efforts are being made to ensure this.

Employers' organisations

The biggest central organisation of employers is the Danish Employers' Confederation, with about 22,500 members in industry, crafts, building and construction, and commerce and services. Member organisations employ about 520,000 people, of which 320,000 are manual workers and the remaining 200,000 are salaried employees. Within the scope of the Danish Employers' Confederation there are about 150 associations of employers representing different trades and geographical areas. The iron and metal industry has the biggest employers' association and accounts for about 35 per cent of the total number of people employed.

The number of member organisations affiliated to the Danish Employers' Confederation has remained more or less constant throughout the 1980s, but there has been a marked growth in the number of workers they employed.

In addition to the Danish Employers' Confederation there are employer organisations for agriculture, and for the financial sector (banks and insurance companies).

In the public sector there are no traditional organisations of employers, but matters related to collective agreements, etc., are co-ordinated by the Association of Municipal Authorities, the Association of County Authorities and the Ministry of Finance.

3. The role of the State in industrial relations

(a) The general biennial renewals of collective agreements since 1973

The collective bargaining rounds in 1973 ended in the conclusion of agreements only after large-scale industrial disputes in the private sector. When the collective agreements came up for renewal in the spring of 1975, the parties were not able to reach agreement, even with the assistance of the Public Conciliator. The Folketing (Danish Parliament) passed legislation designed to restrain increases in income for all major groups in society.

The background to this legislation was that large-scale industrial action would throw a further 350,000 persons into unemployment of unknown duration, that the general uncertainty dampening production and employment would increase, and that an interruption in export production and supplies in the then uncertain situation might have adverse effects which could go far beyond the immediate fall in exports.

On the labour market, the collective agreements were extended for a two-year period, with the changes proposed by the Public Conciliator, in the industries covered by the Danish Employers' Confederation and the Federation of Danish Trade Unions, and with the changes agreed upon by the parties within the limits of the framework laid down in the proposals of the Public Conciliator.

The proposals meant that all employees would be covered by the same flat rate, cost-of-living adjustment scheme. Some, including public employees, had enjoyed a percentage indexation scheme since 1975, and it was possible to agree on wage-drift schemes for these groups (see also below).

In the course of 1976 it became necessary to intervene in economic developments and a broad political majority supported the agreement to restrict increases in incomes for all groups to 6 per cent annually for the period 1976-79, to introduce higher excise duties, to grant support to trade and industry and to initiate employment-promoting and other labour market policy measures.

In this connection the Folketing urged the social partners to negotiate new agreements for 1977-79 with an average increase of 2 per cent a year in addition to cost-of-living indexation, taking into special consideration the lowest paid. The

Folketing asked for any cost-of-living indexation bonus in excess of one per six-month period to be suspended. Instead, the State was asked to pay an amount into the Labour Market Supplementary Pension Fund for each employee (see below).

In the collective bargaining rounds of 1977, however, the central organisations failed to reach an agreement within the framework laid down by the Folketing. A draft settlement proposed by the Public Conciliator for sectors covered by the Danish Employers' Confederation and the Federation of Danish Trade Unions was rejected, and there was a risk that industrial action would paralyse vital social functions and central parts of trade and industry. The Folketing thus decided to pass legislation giving the draft settlement the force of law. Subsequently, agreements were concluded for the remaining sectors.

During the collective bargaining rounds in the spring of 1979, the parties in both the private and public sectors failed to reach agreement on general questions. Notice had been given of industrial action involving about 310,000 employees and including a number of enterprises which would, among other things, disrupt oil supplies, electricity generation, the transport of goods and passenger ferries.

To prevent this industrial action, and thus the serious risk to the national economy and employment, and in order to maintain economic development objectives, the Folketing passed legislation extending the collective agreements already in force for a two-year period. A few changes were made, such as temporary suspension of automatic cost-of-living indexation schemes, an increase in guaranteed minimum wages, and an overall sum for wage improvements, in particular for the low paid. At the same time the holiday period was extended by one week and restrictions on increases in income were imposed on all groups.

The collective agreements were renewed by agreement between the social partners in 1981 after decentralised negotiations.

After elections in 1982 the new Government stated that wage increases for public employees in the agreement period 1983-85 should be kept under 4 per cent a year. It urged the parties in the private sector to conclude agreements taking into consideration the strict curb on incomes elsewhere.

New agreements between the social partners were concluded in the spring of 1983.

The collective bargaining rounds in the spring of 1985 again found the parties unable to reach agreement. Industrial action was taken by about 300,000 employees in the industries covered by the Danish Employers' Confederation and Federation of Danish Trade Unions, while notice of industrial action was given by at least 200,000 employees in other industries.

The action taken affected essential services and halted vital activities of society and industry. The Government felt that the situation might escalate to a point where general welfare would be endangered and yet it regarded the continuation of restrictive economic policies as necessary to improve competitiveness, encourage savings and reduce consumption. Accordingly, it proposed an incomes policy package.

The package included restrictions on income increases for all groups, restrictions on price increases, subsidies for employers' contributions in respect of their employees, a compulsory savings scheme and an increase in corporation tax from

40 to 50 per cent. All collective agreements were extended for two years, with wage increases limited to 3.5 per cent a year. Towards the end of the agreement period, working time was reduced by one hour a week, without loss of pay.

The legislation resulted in a complaint to the ILO from the Federation of Danish Trade Unions and the Danish Federation of Public Servants' and Salaried Employees' Organisations.

The collective agreements were renewed by the social partners in the spring of 1987.

In addition to the general legislation mentioned concerning collective agreements during the period 1973-87, there have been three Acts implementing temporary wage freezes.

(b) Legislative initiatives concerning collective agreements in specific occupations

Since 1975, 11 Acts have been adopted concerning renewal or extension of collective agreements in specific occupations where industrial action was taken or where there was a risk of such action. Five of these agreements deal with working conditions in Greenland.

The remaining six Acts concern collective agreements in occupations of vital importance to society – for example, navigation, hospitals, ambulance services and fire services.

(c) Suspension of the automatic cost-of-living indexation scheme

As mentioned above, the general legislation in connection with the renewal of collective agreements in 1975 meant that the same flat rate cost-of-living adjustment bonus was paid to all groups (as opposed to the previous percentage indexation).

The 1976 resolution of the Danish Folketing concerning incomes policy was accompanied by an understanding that if price increases triggered off more than one cost-of-living bonus in the half-yearly adjustments, then the additional bonus/es should be suspended and the State should instead pay a certain amount per employee per suspended bonus into the Labour Market Supplementary Pension Fund.

In the autumn of 1979 the economic situation was beginning to deteriorate drastically. As an element of national economic policy the Folketing passed legislation to the effect that the indexation for January 1980 (estimated to be two bonuses) should be suspended; bonuses in respect of future six-monthly adjustments in excess of the first were increased; the cost-of-living index was put back to 100; and fuel prices were excluded from the basis for the index calculation.

After the change of Government in 1982, legislation was passed which suspended the cost-of-living scheme up to, and including, the agreement period 1983-85.

The suspension of the cost-of-living indexation scheme was prolonged in 1984 and in the summer of 1986 the Folketing passed an Act under which existing agreements concerning cost-of-living indexation of wages were abolished altogether.

4. The structure and substance of collective bargaining

(a) Central negotiations

For many years collective agreements for industries covered by the Danish Employers' Confederation and the Federation of Danish Trade Unions have been negotiated through a centralised system. The two organisations have bargained on general claims in relation to, for instance, working time, holiday pay, cost-of-living indexation, guarantee pay and duration of agreements. Other (special) claims have been negotiated between the parties to individual agreements, in some cases with the assistance of the central organisations. Typically, general claims have been agreed before special claims are negotiated. The result does not seem to have been influenced by the procedure followed.

In addition to wages determination through central negotiations, wage bargaining may also take place in individual enterprises, for instance in the form of piece-rate or bonus schemes or agreements between the individual employee and the employer.

To some extent centralised negotiations have reflected the Danish labour market structure and, on the employee side, also express the principles of solidarity according to which the Federation of Danish Trade Unions negotiates the key issues.

Details of the negotiation procedure have been laid down by the two central organisations in rules or agreements on negotiating guide-lines (so-called "time-tables").

The agreements mentioned have, among other things, specified time-limits for the negotiations, the distribution of powers between the central organisations and their members concerning negotiations on general and special claims respectively, and rules related to further negotiations with the assistance of the Public Conciliator. The more detailed rules on conciliation are laid down in the Act on Conciliation in Industrial Disputes.

Around 1980 the appropriateness of the central negotiations was discussed. At that time there had been widespread industrial action in the private sector in 1973 and the renewal of collective agreements in 1975, 1977 and 1979 had taken place in whole or in part through legislative initiatives.

It was argued that it was difficult to involve individual employees and individual undertakings due to the gap between "the users of the agreements" and the decision-makers. This lack of involvement is, among other things, reflected in the low voting rates for ballots concerning draft settlements. Dissatisfaction was also expressed with the time-tabling of negotiations of collective agreements.

Some felt that centralised negotiations weakened the possibilities for structural adjustment because of the limited room for manoeuvre given to the negotiating parties.

(b) Decentralised negotiations

The disappointing negotiation results during the 1970s led to a re-evaluation of the bargaining system, and a move in the direction of decentralisation.

As early as 1981 the Danish Employers' Confederation and the Federation of Danish Trade Unions agreed on a decentralised negotiation model according to which collective bargaining was conducted directly between the parties to the individual agreements. Agreement was arrived at in all industries with the exception of the printing industry where three months' industrial action preceded agreement.

New collective agreements were also concluded in 1983 following decentralised negotiations, and agreement was reached in all industries without industrial action being taken.

In 1985 the Federation of Danish Trade Unions and the affiliated unions changed their minds. They felt that due attention had not been given to matters which they considered to be of vital importance in the negotiations in 1981 and 1983. They thus wanted to go back to central negotiations, at least during the initial phase. The parties never got past the initial phase and the result was industrial action for one week at the end of March 1985. The action was ended by legislation, which itself provoked a number of strikes to demonstrate dissatisfaction with such political intervention.

In 1987 agreement could not be reached on a timetable, which meant in principle that the negotiations were completely decentralised, conducted according to the rules laid down in the individual agreements, the Basic Agreement and the rules contained in the Conciliation in Industrial Disputes Act. Subsequently, however, timetables were agreed on for individual industries on the basis of the decentralised model recommended by the employers.

The negotiations in 1987 marked a new era in many respects. For the first time, an agreement was reached on a four-year collective contract instead of one for the traditional two years. It should be noted, however, that mid-term negotiations on pay rates will take place in the spring of 1989. The decentralised renewal of collective agreements in 1987 also disproved the thesis that it is not possible to make progress on key issues in decentralised negotiations. By way of example, a significant reduction in working time was obtained.

(c) Trends in working time

For many years, weekly working time was 40 hours. The above-mentioned legislative intervention in 1985 reduced working time to 39 hours a week from 1 December 1986 in the private sector and from 1 January 1987 in the public sector. The renewed collective agreements in 1987 provide for a reduction of weekly working time in two phases to 37 hours a week by 1990.

(d) Wages and incomes policy

For many trade unions in Denmark, wage demands based on the principle of solidarity have been pursued consistently for the past 25 years. Improvements for the lowest paid have been secured through increases in minimum and normal wage rates. The automatic cost-of-living indexation scheme also contained an element of solidarity. The adjustments during the 1970s were fixed as a flat-rate amount per hour for all groups, which gave the lowest paid a comparatively bigger increase to compensate for price rises.

In addition to demands for a wage policy based on the principle of solidarity, the trade unions have pressed for a guarantee against falling real wages. Up to 1983 the automatic cost-of-living indexation scheme gave workers compensation for price increases of the order of 60-66 per cent on average.

Wages policy in the public sector has to a large extent been patterned on the private sector. Public employees have sought to ensure a parallel development in wages, and an automatic adjustment scheme (the so-called wage drift compensation scheme) was introduced generally in the public sector in 1976.

After the first oil crisis in 1973-74, the Government then in office tried to pursue an incomes policy by means of various instruments, including a short-term wage freeze and suspension of the cost-of-living indexation scheme. A number of financial policy measures were also introduced to reduce purchasing power so as to cut the balance-of-payments deficit.

In the autumn of 1982 a new Conservative-Liberal minority Government came into office. While it introduced a number of incomes policy measures, it also suspended the automatic cost-of-living indexation scheme, which had earlier been changed on several occasions in connection with collective agreements and by legislative intervention, and in 1986 the scheme was fully abolished – on both occasions through legislation. All forms of wage drift compensation were abolished. A waiting day was introduced in connection with sickness benefit. Furthermore, the Government indicated that wage increases in the coming agreement period should be limited to 4 per cent a year.

The collective agreements concluded in the spring of 1983 contained elements to restrain wage increases. In the industries covered by the Federation of Danish Trade Unions and the Danish Employers' Confederation, annual wage rises were limited to 4-4.5 per cent for two years, and the automatic wage drift compensation scheme was reintroduced in a modified form.

In the negotiations in 1985 the Government came to play an important role. After the parties failed to reach agreement, and after a week of widespread industrial action, the Government passed legislation extending the collective agreements for a two-year period, and at the same time a norm of 2 per cent for wage increases was fixed for both 1985 and 1986.

For industries covered by the Danish Employers' Confederation and the Federation of Danish Trade Unions, the average rise in wages was, however, about 5 per cent in both 1985 and 1986. The reason why the norm was exceeded was primarily that the demand for labour in various sectors – especially in building and construction and the technology-intensive sectors of industry – was very strong in 1985 and 1986.

In the public sector the general increase in wages was also fixed at 2 per cent per year and there was a certain improvement in the modified wage drift compensation scheme, which means that public employees receive two-thirds of any increase in private sector wages over and above the norm fixed for the first year. The waiting day for sickness benefit was abolished from 1 January 1987.

5. Conclusion

In view of the economic situation in Denmark, with a high level of unemployment and balance-of-payments problems, the Prime Minister has, in his opening speech to the Folketing, invited the social partners to tripartite discussions.

The Prime Minister has also expressed a wish to enter into a binding tripartite agreement in relation to the mid-term negotiations on pay rates in March 1989. The aim is to improve economic competitiveness and to curb rising consumption through wage moderation on the part of employees in return for a general pension scheme, tax reductions and other improvements.

The organisations have expressed certain reservations about this initiative. Neither the trade unions nor the employers will sign away the responsibility for wage determination through conclusion of collective agreements.

Collective bargaining in Finland: Recent trends and problems

Mr. Teuvo Kallio, National Conciliation Officer, Ministry of Social Affairs and Health

1. Context

Industrial relations in Finland can be briefly described in the following way. Since the beginning of the 1980s Finnish industry has experienced strong pressure to develop high technology at the expense of basic industry. Automation and rationalisation have increased and Finnish industry is fast becoming internationalised.

Manufacturing is, however, still more labour-intensive in Finland than in many other countries, employing over a quarter of the labour force. The biggest industrial employers are the metalworking, engineering and pulp, paper and wood industries, which together occupy 53 per cent of all industrial employees. Measured by GDP, Finland's standard of living is among the highest in the world.

The Finnish economic situation can also be looked at in the light of the following figures:
- unemployment peaked at 7.3 per cent in 1978, the highest rate in 40 years. Since 1978 the unemployment rate has remained at around 5 per cent;
- since 1982 GDP has grown annually by about 3 per cent, a rate higher than the average for other OECD countries;
- the standard of living has risen following a decrease in the rate of inflation from about 12 per cent in 1980-81 to 3.5 per cent in 1986. Real earnings rose by 0.4 per cent in 1980 but by 3.2 per cent in 1986.

2. The repercussions of economic, technological and social developments on workers' and employers' organisations

The degree of unionisation of employees rose rapidly in the 1970s and is today around 85 per cent. The employers are also highly organised. Expertise is at a high level and co-operation between the organisations functions well. Similarly, co-operation between the organisations and the Government is in good order.

The size of the labour force is diminishing. The relative proportion of white-collar workers in industry is increasing, representing nowadays over 50 per cent of all employees. The relative proportions of the labour force in the public sector and in service industries are also increasing. According to the employers, an increase in company-level flexibility requires that the negotiating emphasis should be closer to the workplace.

The changes in the composition of the Finnish labour market are also reflected in negotiations. It has become gradually more difficult to reach mutual agreement on objectives. The Finnish bargaining system is strongly centralised: the number of items included in the collective agreements has grown and disputes on their correct interpretation are solved within the organisations.

3. The role of the State in industrial relations

With the exception of three years, all collective agreements signed since 1968 have been based on incomes policy agreements between the central employees' and employers' organisations and the State. The agreements have covered the private and public sector alike, and they have been valid for one or two years.

The incomes policy agreement for 1984-85, for instance, included pay indexation and a reduction of working hours. Also agreed to under pressure was a ninefold increase of fines in an effort to reduce the thousands of wildcat strikes that occur annually in Finland. An ominous sign was that one of the central organisations, representing academics, abstained from signing the agreement. Strikes by medical practitioners, teachers and others were of very long duration.

The purpose of incomes policy agreements is to promote employment and slow down inflation so as to keep Finland internationally competitive at the same time as increasing real earnings. In the incomes policy negotiations the State plays an active third-party role. Negotiations cover pay, prices, taxes, manpower and social policy and often also agricultural policy.

The negotiations have to be based on precise date on the economy. For this purpose the Governing has set up an Incomes Policy Investigation Committee on which the central organisations are represented. When necessary the Government names an incomes policy officer to co-ordinate negotiations between the organisations and to act as a go-between for the State and the organisations.

In the search for flexibility the mechanism of centralised incomes policy negotiation is coming under increased scrutiny. In 1986, two incomes policy agreements were signed: the first for white-collar workers and the second for blue-collar workers.

In the first half of the 1970s incomes policy proved to be a successful means of maintaining industrial peace but recent experience has shown that incomes policy alone is an inadequate tool for controlling demand. In the long run the present system of incomes policy agreements may cause rigidity in negotiating procedures and impede the solution of specific sectoral problems unless it is continually adapted to changing circumstances. At present there is growing pressure for decentralisation.

Nevertheless, under certain conditions incomes policy can be an effective instrument in economic policy designed to dampen inflation, sustain economic growth and reduce unemployment.

Legally the incomes policy agreement is not binding. It is not a collective agreement including provisions on industrial peace. A commitment to industrial peace is based only upon the social partners' freedom to agree between themselves, not upon coercion by the State.

Generally governments have declared their political will to implement the proposals which the social partners have agreed on concerning the development of legislation related to working life. The nature of political decision-making powers in Parliament – especially the power of a minority – and the large influence of the labour market organisations have usually made governments keen to pursue a so-called consensus policy.

The present Government's programme includes, for example, the development of workers' participation and representation, unemployment security, shorter working hours for parents of small children, the right to refuse dangerous work, and so on.

We should also mention the problems concerning the double role of the State as the public authority on the one hand and as an employer on the other.

4. The structure of collective bargaining

Up to now bargaining has usually started at the central organisation level, with the central organisations trying to reach an agreement on general lines for sectoral agreements. The central agreements are not legally binding but are only recommendations, and the member organisations are entitled to dissociate themselves from them.

In recent years a great deal of criticism has been expressed of the so-called consensus policy in the labour market. The criticism stems from the fact that centralised framework agreements have not secured industrial peace, and that the special circumstances of the various branches have not been taken into account.

The employers have therefore advocated decentralisation towards the sector and company level. The trade unions, however, have pursued the opposite policy. Collective agreements covering only single places of work are possible but rare.

The duration of collective agreements varies between the different sectors. For example, during the past few years the private service sector has pursued its collective bargaining in a manner increasingly independent of industry in terms of both content and timing of the agreements.

It was not until 1970 that a collective agreements system was created in the public sector. Compared with that in the private sector the negotiation system is much more centralised.

5. The substance of collective agreements

The most recent incomes policy agreement was concluded in the spring of 1986. The most important issue was the reduction of working hours for employees then on a 40-hour week.

The question of flexibility has been a key topic in Finland. The reduction of working hours offers a good example: what is the best way to reduce working hours in practice? Besides working hours the employers have advocated greater flexibility, for example, in the areas of geographical and occupational mobility of labour and the encouragement of performance-related remuneration systems.

For their part, the employees have called attention to the need to adjust personal working hours according to, for instance, the social obligations of the family.

Other central issues in incomes policy discussions have included employment policy, social security, employment security, education and family policy. In the future other issues, such as participation, may become increasingly contentious.

6. The climate of collective bargaining: Disputes, co-operation and participation

The number of union-organised legal strikes has not been high. So-called wildcat strikes – lasting perhaps 4-8 hours at single places of work – were quite frequent in the 1970s and at the beginning of the 1980s. More recently their number has dropped (1,800 in 1984 and 900 in 1985). Most of these strikes have occurred in industry.

Since 1970 strikes and lock-outs have been possible in the public sector. They were very rare during the 1970s but have become increasingly frequent and widespread in the 1980s. They have included strikes by nurses, medical practitioners, teachers and civil servants and employees. Owing to the centralised bargaining system in the public sector, the strikes have had far-reaching consequences.

The Co-operation within Companies Act has been applied in Finland since 1979 but it has to be admitted that its impact on labour disputes has not been very strong. At the moment there is a lively discussion going on concerning the development of the co-operation system: will it bring better results on a compulsory or on a voluntary basis? The trade unions demand the former and employers the latter.

Collective bargaining in the Federal Republic of Germany: Recent trends and problems

Mr. Wolfgang Koberski, Department of Labour Law, Federal Ministry of Labour and Social Affairs

1. The context

The description of the general economic and social trends contained in the ILO's background paper for this Symposium is also applicable, to a large extent, to developments in the Federal Republic of Germany. The Federal Republic of Germany is experiencing a phase of price stability and, at the same time, the decline in employment, which was attributable to general economic and structural conditions, has been halted. Since about the middle of 1984, economic growth and employment have been on the increase. Higher employment figures have been recorded especially in sectors showing high productivity; these are also the sectors that have introduced labour-saving technological innovations. This shows that technological progress is not synonymous with the destruction of jobs, but rather that technological innovation, which can enhance the economy's competitiveness, offers an opportunity for safeguarding existing jobs and creating new ones. Nevertheless, there has been no decline in the number of unemployed people in the Federal Republic of Germany, the principal reasons being demographic evolution and the rise in the number of women looking for work. An additional reason is the existence of structural problems in traditional sectors of industry, such as mining and the iron and steel industry.

2. Implications for the parties to collective bargaining

The circumstances referred to above have not, of course, failed to make an impact on the parties to collective bargaining.

The great problem with which the *trade unions* are faced is that they must not only represent employed people but must also take adequately into account the interests of the unemployed. A further problem for the unions is how to recruit young workers and highly skilled employees who account for an increasing share of the total number of persons in employment. In particular, in areas where new technologies are being introduced, the line of demarcation between wage-earning workers and salaried employees is becoming increasingly blurred. It seems that the trade unions are not yet sufficiently prepared for this change in the structure of the labour force.

At the same time, it should be noted that the 17 individual unions affiliated to the German Confederation of Trade Unions (Deutscher Gewerkschaftsbund (DGB)) and the Christian Trade Union Federation were able to report an increase in their membership in 1986, whereas in the case of the German Employees' Union (Deutsche Angestellten-Gewerkschaft) and of the German Civil Servants' Federation (Deutscher Beamtenbund) a slight decline in membership was recorded.

It cannot therefore be said that there has been any weakening of workers' organisations or, consequently, of their bargaining position. The strength of their position is reflected in the results of collective negotiations.

The difficulties facing *employers' organisations,* on the other hand, in their relations with their members, do not seem to be so serious.

The principal point on which some employers criticise their organisations is that, in their view, the concessions made in collective negotiations have been excessive. A further criticism is that the agreements concluded in the course of the collective bargaining process are not sufficiently flexible. The critics argue that the collective agreements should take greater account of regional and technical differences and make greater allowance for variations in return as between different enterprises in the same sector.

Small firms, in particular, complain that their interests are not sufficiently taken into account.

3. The role of the State

The ILO's background paper points out very pertinently that, unlike other governments, the Government of the Federal Republic of Germany eschews any large-scale and persistent intervention in the autonomy of the collective bargaining process.

One characteristic, and possibly a decisive one, of our system of making collective agreements is the non-intervention of the State. In the Federal Republic of Germany, the principle which applies to the elaboration of the conditions governing pay and employment is that of the self-determination of the parties concerned and their organisations. The conditions of employment in question are settled by the organisations themselves on their own responsibility.

This non-intervention on the part of the State is reflected, for example, in the following criteria:

- There are no legislative provisions concerning the structure of workers' and employers' organisations. The Constitution guarantees freedom of association – the right granted to every person to form an association. The employers' and workers' organisations are not subject to any state regulations governing the establishment and activities of such organisations.
- While there are no legislative provisions concerning the recognition of trade unions for purposes of collective bargaining, and while no need for such provisions has so far arisen, the question of the capacity of a trade union to be a party to collective bargaining can be settled by the independent courts. Legal decisions in

such cases are based on general principles evolved by case-law, in particular by the Federal Labour Tribunal.
- There are no legislative provisions concerning the bodies which are to conduct negotiations. It is left to the organisations to incorporate relevant provisions in their own rules and regulations, and this is what happens in most cases.
- There are no legislative provisions concerning the procedure to be followed in collective negotiations. The parties to a collective agreement settle, by virtue of their own competence and on their responsibility, all procedural questions concerning collective negotiations. There has so far been no need for a statutory enactment of rules of procedure.

It should be noted, however, as a qualifying remark, that before collective bargaining takes place and depending on the substance of the claims made by trade unions, the federal Government or certain ministers express their opinion on specific subjects. Nor should it be forgotten that after the CDU/CSU/FDP had become the governing coalition, the first demand made was for a "freeze" on wage increases in order to stimulate the economy. However, this demand was strenuously opposed by the parties to collective agreements, with the result that this move came to nothing. Similarly, while the federal Government had at first been unfavourable to the trend towards a reduction of the standard weekly working time to less than 40 hours, the Government has since taken a more dispassionate approach.

At present there are no formal meetings in the Federal Republic of Germany between the Government and the social partners; such meetings took place in the early 1970s on the basis of the stabilisation legislation enacted as part of the "concerted action" programme at the time. Since 1977, however, this special form of information exchange has been discontinued.

Nevertheless, from time to time, talks take place at the highest government level, and even with the participation of the Federal Chancellor, between the Government and the umbrella organisations of the parties to collective agreements (the Confederation of German Employers' Associations, the German Confederation of Trade Unions, and the German Employees' Union); most recently, such talks have taken place with the German Confederation of Trade Unions on hours of work and tax reform. The object of these talks is to exchange information and to endeavour to reach a minimum consensus on questions of wages and employment policy.

4. *The structure of collective bargaining*

Collective agreements are concluded at various levels. There are no collective agreements at the federal level, i.e. agreements covering all sectors of the economy. However, quite frequently the parties to collective agreements which are concerned with particular sectors of the economy enter into agreements applicable to several regions, or even to the entire territory of the Federal Republic. As a rule, however, collective agreements are regional in scope, that is, they cover specific sectors in one or more of the Länder of the Federal Republic. It is generally at this level that collective wage and salary agreements are concluded, in so far as so-called enterprise-level agreements are not entered into.

Admittedly, there is no evidence to show that in recent years collective bargaining has been carried on to a greater extent at enterprise level than in previous years. As in the past, collective bargaining takes place predominantly at the regional level, not at enterprise level. In the case of certain important areas, such as the public service, the chemical industry and the building industry, collective negotiations are conducted at the federal level.

Nevertheless, even in cases where the negotiations take place at the regional level, the influence exerted by the organisations at federal level makes itself felt, with the consequence (among others) that the regional collective agreements differ only slightly from one another.

A further point to be noted is that, in essential matters, the collective bargaining policy is determined, or at least influenced, by the more powerful trade unions. When these powerful unions succeed in achieving a breakthrough as regards collective bargaining policy, the smaller, less militant unions are guided by the results of such bargaining.

With respect to the points mentioned above, observers have expressed the opinion that a trend towards the decentralisation of collective bargaining is discernible in the Federal Republic of Germany. Actually, it is very doubtful that there is such a trend. At most, what could be said is that there is some evidence of such a trend in the manner by which collective agreements have settled the question of the reduction of the standard weekly working time to less than 40 hours. Pursuant to these agreements, enterprises in sectors covered by the provisions of such agreements have been given greater latitude than in the past to make adjustments in the provisions of collective agreements by means of concluding agreements at enterprise level.

On the other hand, however, it should be noted that the collective agreement concluded this year in the metallurgical industry – which incorporates at the same time a graduated plan for wage increases and reductions of working time for the period up to 1990 – received its final shape as a result of top-level consultations between Gesamtmetall, the industry's umbrella employers' organisation, and IG Metall, the workers' organisation. The subsequent agreements entered into at regional level accepted the compromise and merely supplemented it in certain respects that had to be dealt with at the regional level, such as Saturday work, monthly wage, and similar matters.

According to the opinion expressed recently by Mr. Steinkühler, President of IG Metall, this organisation does not, however, consider that this mode of conducting negotiations reflects a new trend. Rather, it takes the view that, as in the past, collective bargaining must and should be carried on in future at the regional level. This is also the view held by Mr. Stihl, of Baden-Württemberg, who conducted the negotiations on behalf of Gesamtmetall.

5. The substance of collective bargaining

Recent years have been characterised by moderation in the trade unions' claims for wage and salary increases. This moderate attitude may well be attributable to developments in the trade unions' thinking with a view to making their own contribution to the fight against unemployment and to job security.

Instead, the unions have focused their collective bargaining policy on a reduction of hours of work, in particular of weekly working time. However, the parties to collective agreements hold different views as regards the impact on the economy and on employment policy of the greater flexibility of working hours and of the reduction of the standard weekly working time to less than 40 hours.

On the one hand, both sides emphasise that the adjustment of working time can be expected to yield, as one of the results, gains in employment, but the employers stress above all that such gains can be achieved only if more flexible working rules can be simultaneously introduced at enterprise level. The trade unions, and especially IG Metall, take the view, by contrast, that every form of reduction of working time offers a genuine possibility not only of safeguarding jobs but also of creating additional employment opportunities. Accordingly, they interpret the employment statistics in this sense and argue that the majority of the new openings for employment can be ascribed to the reduction of working time.

The federal Government has kept out of this dispute and has merely pointed out that the official statistical data do not offer any clue as to the causes of the rise in employment in recent years. The Government has stated, however, that it expects the flexible working rules to lead to a steady improvement in the employment situation.

6. The climate of industrial relations

The climate of industrial relations can be gauged most readily by reference to developments in the field of industrial action. Apart from the strikes in the metallurgical and printing industries in 1984, the number of workers participating in strikes and affected by lock-outs in the Federal Republic of Germany in the period 1980-86 was limited. The same may be said of the number of working days lost. This may be said to be consistent with international developments, in that the number of labour disputes has declined in nearly all countries since 1980.

From the point of view of the federal Government, the relations between employers and workers and their organisations are stable and characterised by co-operation. One of the factors accounting for this readiness to co-operate may well be the pressures exerted by the international economic situation.

The trade unions and the employers' organisations are no doubt agreed in thinking, as in the past, that the system of collective bargaining offers sufficient flexibility to give both sides an opportunity to state their positions. Any impairment of these opportunities or any state intervention which, according to our conception of the Constitution, might be open to question would be fraught with unforeseeable risks, would tend rather to jeopardise the balance of power of the social partners, and so would make the labour market and industrial relations unmanageable.

In any case, the federal Government is of the opinion that the system of collective bargaining has proved its worth since the establishment of the Federal Republic of Germany. The autonomous fixing of minimum conditions governing remuneration and other working conditions by means of collective agreements, which can take account of the circumstances prevailing in the sector and region concerned, is preferable to wage fixing by the State (even in the form of a minimum wage).

Collective bargaining policy in times of change: Developments in the Federal Republic of Germany

Dr. Klaus Dutti, Chief Executive Officer, Federation of Employers in the Private Banking Sector

Dr. Peter Knevels, Executive Officer, Confederation of German Employers' Associations

1.1. Autonomy in collective bargaining means democracy

For almost four decades we, in the Federal Republic of Germany, have had an autonomous collective bargaining system that corresponds to our democratic state system. This autonomy was shaped decisively by, and evolved in consequence of, the experiences of the 1930s and the events of the post-war period. Both the parties to the bargaining process wish to work out the terms of remuneration and conditions of employment on their own responsibility. In their opinion, the State should intervene as little as possible in this field. Autonomy in collective bargaining has evolved to the point where it has become an indispensable part of our democratic Basic Law, having constitutional status, within a social market economy; indeed, this autonomy may be described as the twin of the social market economy.

1.2. The collective agreement is comprehensive

The idea of the collective agreement has by now been totally integrated into the world of labour in our country. About 40,000 collective agreements are in force in the Federal Republic. Annually about 10,000 collective agreements are terminated and renegotiated. The parties to the agreements have the competence to determine the gross earnings from employment (other than self-employment); at present the aggregate amount of these earnings is nearly 1 trillion Deutschmarks. Hence a wage increase of 1 per cent implies a shift of approximately DM10 billion in financial resources. Working time, leisure and the labour market are the three sides of a triangle, the size and changing shape of which are influenced decisively by collective agreements.

1.3. Responsibility of the social partners

As a consequence, employers' and workers' organisations are given an economic responsibility which must be guided, not least, by considerations of the common good. Accordingly, and quite rightly, the parties to the bargaining process are called upon to act with a sense of responsibility. For this reason, they are often the object of public criticism, for they must expect to be judged by their actions. Any industrial dispute is open to criticism querying the need for the dispute.

Not infrequently, critical comment concerns a wage bargaining policy that would not make sufficient allowance for enterprises suffering from adverse conditions or that would make it impossible to step up the re-employment of unemployed persons. In such cases, the principal issue is the desire for greater differentiation, under the terms of the collective agreement in question, so far as cost-related matters are concerned.

1.4. The indispensable equilibrium in collective bargaining policy

The efficient determination of working and economic conditions by collective negotiations conducted by employers' and workers' organisations on their own responsibility presupposes a reciprocal independence and equilibrium of the parties. Only if this condition is satisfied can these organisations make a contribution, in keeping with their function in the national economy, to the appropriate distribution of the national product, and only in such circumstances can they play a part, consistent with their social policy function, in ensuring a balance of interests and thus social peace.

The fundamental prerequisite of a libertarian pluralist order of society – if it is to work efficiently – is an equilibrium of the major power groups. A situation of equilibrium in autonomous collective bargaining connotes a situation of equilibrium in society and in social policy. The two are undoubtedly linked. The main task of the legislature and of the judiciary is to see to it that this situation of equilibrium is maintained.

2.1. Collective bargaining to become more objective

While from the point of view of the employers' organisations there is no alternative to autonomous collective bargaining, and although on the whole, and despite many a tough test, this autonomy has proved its worth, the techniques and content of collective bargaining should be further reflected upon from time to time.

What is meant by the techniques of collective bargaining is in the first place the style, that is the way in which employers' organisations and trade unions confront each other, whether arguments are put forward realistically or emotionally, and whether industrial action, or the threat thereof, remains the exception, i.e. the last resort.

Unfortunately, what happens again and again is that even in the preliminary stage of negotiations on collective agreements, excessive expectations are aroused prematurely among the employees by hard-line decisions taken by the unions which must *ab initio* be regarded as exaggerated and unrealistic. Even though every expert knows that there are considerable gaps between demands and settlements in the matter of collective bargaining, the consequence is that an acceptable compromise solution in such bargaining becomes much more difficult to achieve later on. The number of negotiating rounds increases, the rounds last longer, and industrial action becomes a possibility.

The autonomy of the collective bargaining process calls for strong and competent unions which are headed by a capable leadership and which, by realistic and timely decisions taken in their own decision-making bodies, keep radical groups within their limits.

The employers' organisations fully recognise trade union activities properly so-called as necessary evidence of the *raison d'être* of unions. And it is clear also that the imminence of industrial action invigorates and strengthens the organisation of the unions. Nevertheless, the unions – which are after all recognised as an element of order in our state and social system – should not stray too far from the area of realistic policy.

2.2. Meaningful conciliation machinery

The settlement of disputes and the joint development of pragmatic solutions concerning collective bargaining policy testify to the common sense and maturity of the parties to the bargaining process. In many cases one element of this is agreement on a well thought-out conciliation procedure for the purpose of resolving acute differences arising in collective bargaining. Admittedly, the employers' and workers' organisations in the Federal Republic of Germany have not reached a stage comparable to that of the neighbouring coalitions in Switzerland which, ever since the late 1930s, by virtue of a peace agreement, have voluntarily renounced industrial action. On the other hand, it would be wrong to demand a statutory ban on strikes and lock-outs, for autonomy in collective bargaining and industrial action are objectively interlinked. At most, what the State can do is to create a sensible framework to support the balance of power of the coalitions. In many instances, where negotiations have reached a critical point, the fact that the parties to collective bargaining were able to have recourse to a conciliation procedure led to the clarification and settlement of disputes. In such cases, independent conciliators were able, by their proposals for a settlement, to contribute to the solution of problems.

A question to be considered in the future would be whether, and to what extent, conciliation procedures in specific areas covered by collective bargaining could be developed further, especially in areas where the risk of industrial action has beeen highest. In this connection, the duty to observe industrial peace, and to continue to observe it for a longer period, might acquire special significance, and logically this duty would also have to apply to so-called warning strikes.

3.1. Area of tension between the collective agreement and the enterprise

An important topical subject as regards the scope of collective agreements concerns the regulatory function of these agreements and the limitations thereof. The issue here is whether the collective agreement, by virtue of its content, should so far as possible cover and definitely determine all the conditions of employment in enterprises, or should merely constitute a framework to be further refined and developed at enterprise level. Other points under discussion concern the territorial and occupational coverage and scope of validity of collective agreements, i.e. whether the collective agreement should apply equally to all regions and to all branches or sectors of an industry, or whether the employers should be given the opportunity of negotiating differential wages and other conditions of employment, in the light of the particular firm's profitability and the labour market situation, and according to more individual points of view.

The consideration behind this observation is that critics from the political and academic world, and from among the ranks of employers, query the results of our collective negotiations as being too general and giving equal minimum conditions of employment for all. In particular, in the light of the high unemployment figures and poor earnings of enterprises, they consider that there ought to be more marked wage differentials.

3.2. The collective agreement as an exclusive instrument, or acceptable remuneration for all

There is no doubt that, for economic reasons, some differentiation should be made at enterprise level, not only between sectors of industry and regions but also, and above all, on account of occupational qualifications – and in this respect greater allowance must be made for differences in the demands made on the people concerned and their performance. This requirement can be satisfied most readily by a wage and collective bargaining policy that once again takes greater account of the legal situation, viz. that the conditions of employment laid down in the collective agreements are essentially minimum conditions of employment which are acceptable for all enterprises.

It used to be possible, by means of genuine minimum conditions of employment, to set standards applicable to small, medium and large enterprises in different sectoral and regional situations. On this basis a broader range of working conditions, exceeding those laid down in collective agreements, was built up. To these were added the many and varied kinds of social benefits granted at enterprise level. To this extent, the standard-setting function of the collective agreements and the scope for adaptation at enterprise level were in a balanced relationship.

This relatively large gamut of conditions of employment, varying from one enterprise to another, gave rise within the unions as long ago as the mid-1950s to discussions on "enterprise-linked collective bargaining policy". Its object was to take full advantage of the possibilities offered by collective agreements by means of arrangements varying from one enterprise to another. The only caveat was that the spread of wages above those stipulated in the collective agreement should be kept as small as possible. The employers' organisations – although often only after considerable initial resistance – agreed to go along, all the more because in times of economic boom and full employment it was easier to follow this course and so to consent to excessively high wage awards. A critical reappraisal of the situation became imperative as a result of stagnation, recession and a change in the labour market.

3.3. Need for greater differentiation in the collective bargaining policy

What is needed is a return to a moderate policy in the negotiation of collective agreements, geared essentially to the performance potential of all enterprises in the industrial sector to which the agreements apply. The possible margins of apportionment should concentrate primarily on the wage, and the additional wage costs should be limited.

By contrast with first impressions, there have always been – and there will also be in future – more or less great differentials in conditions of employment under collective agreements, and in cases where terms superior to those of the agreements applied, depending on sectoral or regional criteria, between particular branches of industry or between areas covered by the agreements. These differentials might be further developed. Already the collective agreements concluded in the period 1984-87 show a considerable range of percentages and generally a return to a more pronounced differentiation in the conditions of employment stipulated in the agreements. The wage increases provided for in the agreements must be structured in such a way as to allow the enterprises a sufficient margin – over and above the rates specified in the agreements – within which differentials may be applied according to skill, sector and location.

3.4. General regulation through collective agreements, not fragmentation

It follows that the key issue in a policy of wage differentials must be what possibilities exist for differentiation in the real world, for there are limits to wage differentiation under collective agreements – for example, if an excessively sharp differentiation of agreed wages jeopardises the regulatory function of collective agreements in the economy and in society as a whole. Accordingly, a middle course has to be sought between a differentiating collective bargaining policy that takes account of the diverse situations and an excessive standardisation of the policy.

For the purpose of maintaining the peace-making function of collective agreements, the binding nature of the standards set out in the agreements as minimum conditions of employment should not be questioned. For this reason it is no permanent solution to stipulate in collective agreements regulatory clauses making it possible, in particular firms and at enterprise level, to agree on amendments to the agreements and to agree on lower – though possibly also higher – wages than those provided for in the general agreements, for such clauses impair the credibility and validity of the provisions of the collective agreements and involve the enterprises and organisations in endless discussions about wages. In emergency cases affecting individual enterprises, corrective action might be taken through arrangements between the parties to the collective agreement concerned.

Consequently, the collective agreement should not lose its general regulatory function in the future, for so far as the enterprises are concerned the collective agreement remains a reliable basis for their calculations. A more far-reaching differentiation of the cost structure of enterprises in analogous situations might lead to undesirable distortions of competition. An excessive fragmentation of existing wage structures by means of arrangements made in particular sectors or firms would tend to result in a fragmentation of collective bargaining policy. This would be incompatible with the principles and requirements of co-ordination of wages and bargaining policy, corresponding to the overriding considerations of the national economy. A wages policy geared predominantly to the enterprise would lead to the break-up of the coalitions. The common attitude with respect to collective bargaining policy would be compromised.

4.1. Hours-of-work policy at a turning point

For the trade unions the next most important subject in the context of collective bargaining policy, after wages, is the length of working time. Over a period of decades a more rational scheduling of work and an improved organisation of work made it possible to carry out the work available in the national economy, even though, as a result of collective agreements, working time was becoming shorter. Now the stage has been reached at which cost and practical considerations put a limit to this process.

The main problems affecting progress towards shorter working time are the increased labour costs that have to be absorbed and loss of working capacities in the case of certain groups of workers. While the shorter working week, longer leave and a shorter working life are formally three different things, their effect is to a large extent the same.

Compared with the rest of the world we have "won" the leading position in the statistics on shortest working time, if all leave and other kinds of time off are added together. It would now be sensible to allow a breathing space of some duration.

The controversies concerning the shortening of the 40-hour working week provided for in the collective agreements have shown clearly that now, and even more in the future, new approaches will have to be adopted and that novel methods of regulating working time by collective agreement are indispensable, if we are not to lose sight of the constant targets of the national economy – adequate growth, sufficient employment and price stability. The question is how to absorb the labour costs which are rising in consequence of new developments in collective agreements and how to make these higher costs tolerable. It must be made possible to make longer use of high-quality and highly technological labour resources – which add to capital costs – if the share of capital in the product is not only not to increase, but rather – for the sake of productivity and competitiveness – is to be reduced. This consideration, however, is a cogent argument in favour of longer operating hours. Operating hours and working hours will tend more and more frequently to diverge.

This is the background of the idea of flexible working time as a new development in collective bargaining policy (see section 4.2 for details).

4.2. Flexible organisation of working time

In 1984, after protracted industrial action, the employers consented to a shortening of the 40-hour week in several sectors of the economy, after agreement had simultaneously been reached on a flexible organisation of working time. Regardless of these developments – which continued in 1987 – the fundamental objections (referred to above) to across-the-board and general reductions of working time remain valid. However, in so far as exceptions depend on the situation in collective bargaining policy, it would be wrong to waive the possibility of organising working time as flexibly as possible, with due regard for the exigencies of the enterprise.

Irrespective of what has been said above, flexible working time will in any case be the working time of the future. Rigid contractual regulations will be progressively less capable of taking account of modern methods of production. The collective agreement of the future is likely to get further and further away from the notion of a fixed working time for all workers. It will probably become increasingly rare in the next few decades for one and the same working time to apply uniformly to all enterprises within the scope of a collective agreement. The collective agreement of the future will have to accord to workers and to enterprises a broader range of possibilities for organising working time.

The enterprise's need for flexible systems of working time corresponds to the workers' desire to plan their own individual lives. The better the needs of the enterprise and the workers' personal interest are attuned to each other, the greater are the advantages for both.

The criteria are: efficiency on the enterprise side and acceptance on the human side. Greater flexibility and differentiation in the conditions of employment do not signify any impairment of social protection but imply, rather, a new and more meaningful way of shaping the statutory, collective and individual contract of employment.

Hours of work and the operating hours of enterprises cannot be forced into a single uniform pattern. Competitive production, high wage costs, short average working hours and the supply of manpower demand the optimum utilisation of the enterprise's capacities and machinery. Flexible conditions of working time take these requirements into account. Progress along these lines must continue.

Flexible working times keep costs under control, and this contributes to ensuring and reinforcing the competitiveness of the enterprises. The reduction of down-time and the avoidance of expensive overtime supplements, thanks to a flexible adjustment of working time to the volume of work, save costs and raise the productivity of labour. In addition, by means of an extension of the enterprise's operating hours, it becomes possible to improve the return on the capital invested independently of the individual working times. The two together secure existing jobs and create new employment opportunities.

Across-the-board reductions of weekly working time with full wage adjustment do not promote employment; they hamper employment. Increased employment by contrast, is fostered by ideas of working time that dissociate themselves from rigid methods of scheduling working time and so minimise the enterprise's economic costs. The broader the range of flexible work schedules, the greater will be the benefit for both workers and enterprises. Trade unions must not close their minds to these considerations.

5.1. Technology and collective bargaining policy

Technical progress must serve to enhance the competitive capacity of the economy. Furthermore, new techniques also ensure improved working and living conditions, and a better ecological environment. Technology and technical structural change improve our position in the international markets and are an important prerequisite for the creation of new jobs and the maintenance of existing ones. The present high level of unemployment cannot be attributed to technological factors. While it is true that to some extent new technologies may make certain jobs superfluous, they do, however, at the same time offer scope for creating new or different jobs and services. As competitive capacity is strengthened, jobs will be created in industry and with structural change an information and service society will evolve. All long-term forecasts indicate that the biggest future growth in employment will occur in the communications and service sectors. This means that it is too little – not too much – technology that is fraught with the greater risk.

Another point to be taken into account in future collective bargaining policy is that in many cases the new technology involves a change in traditional skill characteristics. In the context of such changes the level of skill rises for the majority of the workers. This has been recognised by enterprises in the course of the action taken by them to promote training and further training. These initiatives and developments are of course reflected in adjusted job evaluations, and are provided for in collective agreements, in the relevant provisions concerning wages and salaries.

It is part of the modern management of enterprises that workers and works councils should be informed fully and in good time of the proposed introduction of technological innovations. The people employed in the enterprises want to and ought to know what their position is. The provision of such information allays fears and removes a sense of insecurity. The sense of responsiblity on the part of enterprises, the Works Constitution Act and the legislation concerning co-determination at enterprise level go a long way towards ensuring that the workers' social interests are taken into account when technological changes are introduced. Workers, like the population generally, are highly receptive to technology.

In this connection the trade unions demand an enlargement of the works councils' statutory rights of co-determination, either through the enactment of fresh legislations or through collective agreements. In their opinion, technological investments and innovations in working methods should be made subject to the approval of the union concerned, of the works councils and, where appropriate, of the conciliation office. They consider in particular that the planning and implementation of ratification measures should be subject to the agreement of workers' representatives, and that the existing rights of co-determination of works councils should be enlarged for this purpose.

Such a step would impair the employers' freedom to decide on the introduction of technological innovations and would be bound to block investments in enterprises. In a free market economy the right to make economic decisions on fundamental matters affecting the enterprise must, in the final analysis, remain in the hands of the management, for it is the managers who are answerable for the risk involved in the investment policy. The tasks facing enterprises as a result of technological progress can only be dealt with successfully if the initiative and innovative resources of enterprises can be deployed without any restriction. Collective bargaining policy should not interfere in this domain.

5.2. Wages policy aimed at employment

The wages policy of recent years – which on the whole can be regarded as moderate – was successful from the point of view of employment and social policy. It contributed substantially towards the defeat of inflation, to the strengthening of competitiveness and to the creation of new jobs. One further contributory factor is the longer period of validity of collective agreements, as provided for in the 1987 agreements. At the same time, it allowed the possibility of a rise in incomes. This wages policy has yielded greater benefits for society and for the workers than any exaggerated wages policy could have done. There is no better course than that followed by a wages policy aiming at stability. By the same token such a course offers a margin for the creation of more employment opportunities. Both common sense and a sense of responsibility demand that the parties to collective agreements should continue to follow this course.

The inter-relationship of the level of wages, return on capital, investment and employment has become more than evident during the 1980s. In the early years of the decade, steep wage increases under collective agreements were responsible for drastic declines in investment and heavy job losses. Since 1983 the wage rates have moderated and capital investment by enterprises has risen considerably. Since 1984 employment has resumed its growth, and the number of employment opportunities has increased precisely in those sectors in which the return on capital has evolved particularly favourably. This is unambiguous confirmation of the truth of the saying "The profits of today are the investments of tomorrow and the jobs of the day after tomorrow".

As regards workers' incomes the moderate wages policy has likewise proved its worth. By contrast with the early 1980s, when steep wage increases were nullified by high rates of inflation, the moderate wage rates led to a substantial rise in real incomes at the beginning of the second half of the 1980s.

The bargaining strategy of the unions, aimed at achieving higher employment through a reduction of working time, is fundamentally wrong (see section 4 above). The experience acquired in the meantime shows that employment depends primarily on the general economic situation and not on changes in average working time. Independently of reductions in working time, employment has increased exclusively in sectors and regions that have achieved vigorous growth of ouput. Moreover, additional workers are being recruited above all by those enterprises which have made use of the new possibilities offered by collective agreements for introducing flexible work schedules.

It remains the continuing task of collective bargaining policy to take advantage of opportunities opened up in the field of employment policy. For this purpose, the existing differentiation of wages should be developed further and the wage structure should be geared more closely to skill. This objective can best be achieved if the framework laid down in the collective agreement leaves sufficient margin for the differentiation of net wages at enterprise level. A further incentive for employment would be the introduction of a rate for new entrants in the case of new employment relationships. By contrast, an equalisation of the wage structure through the excessive increase of the lower wage groups impairs recruitment opportunities (see also section 3 above).

To improve the employment situation further and to curb the clandestine economy, it is urgently necessary to stabilise supplementary personnel costs. At the present level, where they account for 80 per cent of the direct remuneration, they represent a very heavy burden for enterprises. As compared with the situation in other countries, enterprises in the Federal Republic of Germany have to bear far heavier supplementary personnel costs. In recent times the charges prescribed by legislation have proved to add greatly to costs. It is equally necessary, however, to avoid any further rise in supplementary personnel costs under collective agreements at enterprise level.

6.1. Tests for judging collective bargaining policy

Good industrial relations are not in the realm of Utopia, because of the difficulties involved in establishing such relations and because of the divergence of interest between the parties. It is true, however, that, despite ideological contrasts and differences due to the interests involved on either side, the image of society in the Federal Republic of Germany has been shaped by co-operation between the social partners. The successes achieved in the quest for an objectively just solution have benefited all concerned. So far, it has been possible to settle working and economic conditions on the sole responsibility of the parties and without the intervention of the State. So far, it can be recorded as a success that, in general and to a very great extent, social peace has been maintained in our country.

A great deal remains to be done in the field with which the social partners are fundamentally concerned – that of collective bargaining policy. The developments in the policy concerning working time, including the possible and necessary measure of introducing flexible working time, will have to be thought out more thoroughly and reflected in the techniques of collective bargaining, in order that workers and enterprises should not encounter difficulties in the practical application of the provisions of the collective agreements. A further point to be considered is in what framework and to what extent the protective function of the collective agreements and individual latitude can be adjusted more closely to practical requirements in the delimitation of working conditions. The motto which should guide collective bargaining policy in the future is that there should be as much collective agreement as necessary and as much latitude as possible.

At the present time the trade unions are clearly at a turning point. In many cases, certain industrial unions are dominated by unilateral partisan thinking and by radical tendencies. Not a few unions are embarking on a disastrous course for fear of suffering a loss of membership. Unemployment is not an environment capable of producing a healthy social climate. For this reason it is a common task of all concerned in our society to eliminate unemployment, and in this context a decisive meaning must be attached to collective bargaining policy. The criterion by which collective bargaining policy will be judged is whether it produces solutions supported by universal consensus.

Collective bargaining in the Federal Republic of Germany: Recent trends and problems

Mr. Joachim Kreimer de Fries, German Confederation of Trade Unions (Deutscher Gewerkschaftsbund (DGB)), Department of Collective Bargaining Policy of the Confederation's Executive Committee

Comments of the trade union side on the paper of the International Labour Office and on the report of Wolfgang Koberski, Government representative (Federal Ministry of Labour and Social Affairs)

1. The context

The increase that has taken place since 1985 in the number of people employed in enterprises is definitely accounted for by the reduction of working time and the upward trend of the economic cycle since 1983. This does not mean, however, that the supra-cyclical trend towards the destruction of jobs has been halted or that the structural crisis of capital accumulation has been eliminated. It is to be feared that in the coming recession hundreds of thousands of jobs will again be lost, some of them permanently.

The race to introduce technological innovations, in response to the pressures of domestic and international competition, cannot be avoided by individual enterprises or by national economies, but under the existing conditions of growth of the capitalist economy, technological change does not lead automatically to an increase in employment; in the *economy as a whole* it is more likely to tend to *reduce the number of jobs.* For this reason it is more necessary than ever to organise work along social lines, to reduce working time, and to manage the economy and technology democratically for the sake of enhancing employment and the quality of life.

2. The repercussions on the workers' organisations

The fall in membership of unions affiliated to the German Confederation of Trade Unions was limited to 3.7 per cent in the years 1982 to 1984, and since then the membership figures have recovered somewhat. The evolution in the size of the membership may perhaps be attributed to the change in the number of persons in employment. It is worth noting incidentally that the renewed growth since 1984 is accounted for by a more than proportional entry of women into the unions (as has been the case of increases in membership generally since 1970), though it should be pointed out that the proportion of female trade union members – 23 per cent or 1.8 million – in the total of 7.8 million members of the unions affiliated to the Confederation still does not correspond to the proportion of women in the total number of persons in employment. Hence, further efforts should be made to promote the active participation of women as union officials at all levels of the trade union organisation.

A further problem arises from the shift in the employment structure away from wage-earning workers and towards salaried employees. Despite encouraging indications of a certain mobilisation among salaried employees, there has not so far been a breakthrough by the unions in this organisational area. The organisational effort continues to lag seriously behind in small firms and in the private service sector, where employment has risen in recent years.

Various inquiries indicate that about 10 per cent of the workers and employees who are not as yet organised are in principle favourably disposed to joining a union, especially in cases where technological change is modifying the working environment. Admittedly, this additional potential cannot be integrated or mobilised straight away within the existing structure, for these potential members include part-time workers and persons whose occupation is subject to wide fluctuations. The trend towards the erosion and a decline of normal working relationships has not yet come to a halt. In this connection, one of the important issues is whether organisational ideas (e.g. concerning policies on working time) are appropriate, and a second issue is how other groups of workers (e.g. skilled employees and young people) can be encouraged to become unionised. It is undoubtedly a key task for the future of the trade union to urge young workers of both sexes to join the organisation and to enlist their co-operation.

Despite problems as regards the future that remain unresolved, trade unions in the Federal Republic of Germany have shown themselves capable of striking and since 1984 have succeeded in obtaining reductions of working time of various kinds. In this way it was possible to safeguard not only the protection provided by the collective agreements but also the capacity to contribute to the shaping of social policy. Nevertheless, or precisely for this reason, it should be noted that the socio-economic and political conditions affecting the organisation and authority of trade unions have *worsened* in consequence of structural adjustment, a chronic economic crisis, mass unemployment and a neo-conservative government policy.

3. The role of the State

I should like to supplement Mr. Koberski's comments on this subject by drawing attention to an important and delicate matter which, in the opinion of the trade unions, reflects badly on the trade union and social policy of the Christian-Liberal Government coalition, viz. the weakening of the competence and capacity of the trade unions in collective bargaining as a result of action taken by the State (in consequence of the amendment, in the spring of 1986, of section 116 of the Employment Promotion Act).

The effect of this legislative measure will be that, in the case of industrial action in connection with a dispute concerning a regional collective agreement, workers in enterprises outside the region in question that are affected indirectly by the repercussions of the strike or lock-out will, under certain conditions, be debarred from drawing their unemployment benefit. The subject is too complex to be set out and discussed in detail in the present context; in the Federal Republic of Germany it has given rise to a vehement political and social controversy that has stirred public opinion.

In our opinion, the events leading up to this anti-union measure include the attempt (which ended in failure) to withhold payment of unemployment benefit, allegedly on the basis of earlier legislation, from the more than 300,000 workers who had been indirectly affected by the industrial action carried out in 1984 in order to achieve a reduction of working time – that is, workers affected by a "cold lock-out".

After this experience, the Government coalition, acting in response to pressure exerted by the employers' organisations, intensified the effectiveness of lock-outs by means of the legislative enactment referred to and in so doing has given the employers a new weapon, but on the other hand has appreciably weakened the striking capacity of the trade unions – in particular that of IG Metall (the metalworkers' union) – eroded the right to strike and made it more difficult for the unions to press their claims.

Reacting to this impairment of their bargaining strength, the unions affiliated to the German Confederation of Trade Unions have substantially reinforced their solidarity, especially in the fight for shorter working time and against lock-outs, and have in addition enlisted the support of other social groups for this purpose. As a consequence, in the context of the round of negotiations concerning working time in the metallurgical and printing industries a sharp clash, that would have involved "hot" and "cold" lock-outs and the corresponding social repercussions for those affected, was successfully avoided in 1987. The fact remains, nevertheless, that the deterioration of the conditions for industrial action (resulting from the amendment to section 116 of the Employment Promotion Act) greatly encumbers the future of trade unions.

4. The substance of collective bargaining

The German Confederation of Trade Unions does not regard it as one of the tasks of the unions engaged in collective bargaining to curb the growth of labour costs or the growth of earnings from employment, let alone to freeze or lower these earnings. Nor do we regard this – at least in the Federal Republic – as an appropriate or socially adequate instrument for maintaining existing jobs or creating new employment opportunities. Accordingly, the modest wage increases of recent years and the losses of real earnings in the years 1981 to 1985 are not attributable to a moderation, supposedly based on such considerations, displayed by the unions in putting forward their wage claims in the course of collective negotiations. The reason is rather the worsening of the socio-economic conditions under which the unions have pressed their claims, particularly their wage claims.

One can at most speak of deliberate (and at the same time qualified) moderation on the trade union side in the matter of wage claims in so far as the cost effect of shorter working time that has an employment effect is taken into account in the level of the wage claim submitted. A direct connection between moderation in the matter of wages and the unions' employment policy exists only in cases where moderation is linked to the reduction of working time. There are also other considerations which explain why the trade unions' collective bargaining policy is

focusing increasingly on qualitative objectives which transcend the general quantitative wages policy. It is focusing on:
- the reduction of working time and its social implications (insufficiently characterised by the term "flexibility", which is open to an interpretation in the opposite sense);
- the question of a more just and more meaningful formation of the wage structure, related to skill and to the characteristics of the activity;
- questions concerning the preservation and further development of skills in keeping with changes in the world of labour;
- the social aspects of technology and the organisation of work.

The discussions in the trade unions about the tasks of collective bargaining policy have, in addition, given rise in the Federal Republic to new initiatives and major agreements in these areas. (Further particulars will be given in the course of the debate on specific subjects.)

Collective bargaining in Italy: Recent trends and problems

Tiziano Treu, Professor of Labour Law at the University of Pavia

Over the last ten years Italian labour relations have proved to be far more flexible than many expected. The process of adjustment has been remarkable and has affected all the actors, including trade unions. The role of the actors, the techniques, the levels and the objectives of adjustment show some peculiarities if compared with those of other European systems. They also show a significant evolution in the passage from a first phase (1975-83) of heavy industrial restructuring to the recent economic prosperity which some consider as a second economic miracle (after that of the 1960s).

1. Consequences for the actors

The changing economic environment and composition of the workforce have affected trade unions' position and strategy more than those of the employers and their associations. Indeed, employers have never been so active in labour relations as in the last few years. They have challenged union legitimacy at times to the point of advocating an "individualisation" of labour relations, with trade unions marginalised if not excluded. A different approach has, however, been taken by public corporations and also by large private firms which are more inclined to offer the unions a "participative" role. A prime example is the IRI agreement (December 1984) which lays down a comprehensive set of procedures for workers' participation in various areas, the most noteworthy being the restructuring and reorganisation of the IRI group with a view to restoring its competitiveness and profitability. The basic trade-off is similar to that of other experiments in participation or consultation at both the central and the enterprise levels: the trade unions agree to facilitate reorganisation by exercising economic self-restraint and helping to promote increased labour flexibility and productivity, while management agrees to involve the employees and their representatives in the process and to adopt labour policies aimed at maximising job security and employment.

However, the contrast between these different management attitudes has become less dramatic. A pragmatic adjustment between management and unions, with more participation and less bargaining, is noticeable in many enterprises.

Trade union membership has been affected by labour market changes but less dramatically than in other countries. Union membership has dropped from its 1978 peak of around 54 per cent of the total workforce to 47 per cent in industry and 53 per cent in the public service. The private service sector is – and has always been – the least organised, at 24 per cent in 1983. This relative stability has been favoured by still widespread public support for unionisation. Moreover, the trade unions are represented in central and local public institutions, including social security bodies, labour market agencies, price control boards, and vocational training and retraining organisations.

The appeal of the traditional trade union message is, however, on the wane among blue-collar workers, among medium- and upper-level white-collar workers who are barely organised outside the public service[1] and even more so among supervisory staff and "new professions" in general. The supervisory staff are partially organised in associations somewhat similar to trade unions, though they do not admit it. The new professions are growing outside trade union influence. Finally, the large small-enterprise sector appears increasingly harder to organise, not only because of the size of the workplace but also because of the "direct" relationship existing therein between employers and employees.

These factors, more than the age gap, are the most serious challenges for trade union representatives. Youngsters may take more time to organise than in the past, but by the age of 25-30 the decisive factor in unionisation again becomes their profession and their position in productive units.

The employers are clearly on the offensive in this respect. A well-known "manifesto" issued by *Federmeccanica* (the major employers' association in the metal industry) openly denounced the inadequacy of traditional trade union policies (collectivism and egalitarianism in particular) to meet the needs of an increasingly diverse and educated workforce and advocated an "individualisation" of labour relations.

While intra-labour movement conflicts are fermenting, they have yet to surface. The supervisory staff in both the private and public sector openly criticise the wage policy of the major trade union confederation as still too egalitarian. However, their associations lack the strength to bargain collectively; instead, individual or group wage increases unilaterally granted by employers are reopening wage differentials.

There are also reports of tension between private and public sector unions, controlled with some difficulty by the main union confederations, with public sector unions complaining of penalisation by the centrally bargained incomes policy. In fact, the 1970s saw a reduction in wage differentials which were previously in favour of the public sector, followed by a fairly balanced trend with some fluctuation in the first half of the 1980s. A few independent unions in the public sector have been quite active and show some gains in membership, particularly among medium- and high-level employees. Their use of the strike weapon has, however, been widely criticised by public opinion and political parties. Self-regulation codes for strikes have been adopted and improved on the initiative of the main confederations and grudgingly followed by the independent unions. Furthermore, Act 93 of 1983, on bargaining in the public sector, requires the adoption of self-regulation codes as a condition for admission of union negotiators to the bargaining table.

It is difficult to forecast how the trade unions will cope with these problems. The leadership continues to examine the situation but new initiatives have been slow to emerge. The CISL (largely Catholic) and UIL (chiefly socialist and social

---

[1] Estimates for 1973-74 gave organisation rates of not more than 36 per cent in the industrial sector, 6 per cent in the commercial sector and 80 per cent in the public service.

democratic) trade union confederations are trying to present themselves as more sensitive than the CGIL (communist and socialist) confederation to the needs of the new working class on matters such as wage policy, employee involvement and workers' participation. Their policy platform encompasses:

- more attention to new professions, improvement of productivity and quality of production;
- more highly differentiated wage structures;
- less weight to general wage increases and more to working time reduction and labour flexibility;
- a less ideological and conflictual approach to labour problems;
- in general, more emphasis on the role of trade unions as providers of services to members in the labour market and at the local community level (CISL now speaks of the trade union as a "social entrepreneur").

It is uncertain how these intentions will be implemented and how competition among the union confederations will develop. Certainly a new pragmatism can be seen in the behaviour of all the trade unions (including CGIL) at the decentralised level, going well beyond stated policy objectives.

One factor behind the trade unions' relative stability is their massive presence in public institutions (particularly, institutions administering social security, labour mobility and vocational training). This institutional presence has strengthened the unions' authority vis-à-vis employees and has helped them to retain some influence within the network of small firms (which are virtually impossible to reach through direct organisational efforts).

2. The role of the State

In the post-war period the State has played a relatively small role in Italian industrial relations, particularly in the light of European traditions. From the mid-1970s to the mid-1980s, however, state involvement increased as part of policy packages to tackle the economic crisis and reduce inflation. State intervention was decisive in arriving at the tripartite agreements of 1977, 1983 and 1984, the main contents of which were the control of wage bargaining and escalator clauses, and a series of economic policies designed to promote employment and labour market flexibility. These experiments in tripartite concertation resulted in a sharp centralisation of Italian industrial relations, and increased some rigidities (for example, by introducing legal control on wage bargaining). They also heightened the tense social and political climate of the country, to the point of provoking a major political confrontation in 1985 when the Communist Party organised a popular referendum against the government decree freezing the escalator clause.

At the same time, other developments were moving in a different direction. Legislative measures agreed in advance by the parties, aimed at reducing some traditional rigidities in the Italian labour market: night work by women, use of temporary and part-time workers, incentives for enterprise transfers, tighter controls on absenteeism, reduction and reorganisation of working time and tentative moves to promote labour mobility in public enterprises.

These innovations, which have become increasingly widespread during the 1980s, indicate a reversal of previous trends in two main directions, now common to the labour relations systems of most market economy countries – decentralisation and greater flexibility. But although they would seem to imply less state involvement in industrial relations, this involvement has not been entirely abolished. Similarly, decentralisation has not been pushed to the point of suspending central bargaining, though the central agreement of May 1986 was less loaded with macro-economic measures than the tripartite agreements of 1983-84, and was rather more flexible. General guide-lines were set to keep wage increases in line with inflation, but they did not preclude decentralised bargaining for wage increases above the expected level of inflation. In fact, in the 1987 national bargaining round, wages rose 1.5-2 per cent beyond the 4.5 per cent target, and higher increases are likely in the round of enterprise bargaining now beginning. After years of stagnation of real wages, these increases have begun to encroach on the gains from actual and expected productivity growth.

A similar pattern of flexible guide-lines for collective bargaining has emerged in the public sector, though the justification on productivity grounds of wage increases greater than the inflation rate is highly dubious. The central agreement of 1986 was formally bipartite, contrary to the typical pattern of tripartite social concertation. But government intervention was still important in supporting the negotiation between the parties, basically offering the same incentives used in some previous agreements (such as reducing fiscal drag on wages, cutting social security contributions and improving employment support policies).

While involvement in industrial relations is more informal and less wholehearted than in the past, government policies continue to favour a consensual and, in some form, socially controlled evolution of industrial relations on the grounds that the political cost of outright market liberalisation would be insupportable. State involvement has helped reassure the trade unions and promoted a positive attitude towards industrial restructuring. It has also been a restraining influence on the more extreme factions of employers and a stabilising factor for the whole industrial relations system.

3. *The structure of collective bargaining*

It has already been mentioned that collective bargaining has become more decentralised in the last few years. But the decentralisation process is still held back, not only by confederal agreements but also by national industry-wide bargaining. Although bargaining at the industry level – traditionally the most important in Italy as in other European countries – has been losing ground, forecasts of its total decline have proved wrong. The value of industry-wide bargaining as a stabilising factor in labour relations is still recognised by both employers and trade unions. The wage round of 1987, concluded with unprecedented speed and relatively little conflict, has confirmed the key importance of this bargaining level.

A further aspect of decentralisation of the bargaining structure that is peculiar to Italy is the intermediate level of labour relations between the industry and the enterprise, namely the local-territorial level. At this level – unevenly effective in the past – the social partners and the regional/provincial governments have been increasingly active in the attempt to solve labour market problems arising from industrial restructuring. Tripartite institutions, mostly at regional level, play a key role in promoting professional training and retraining redundant workers, and in administering a large part of the public funds for employment programmes. This local-territorial level has played an essential role in implementing the "controlled" move towards greater labour market flexibility decided by central agreement and partly sanctioned by legislation. Most of this legislation does not in fact increase employers' discretion in the use of manpower, but delegates decisions on flexibility to bipartite or tripartite bargaining groups at enterprise level. For this reason the existence of the "meso" level of labour relations has helped both to reduce the overload on the central tripartism of the 1970s and to reinforce the reassuring effect of public policy, particularly vis-à-vis the trade unions.

The decentralisation process has been particularly difficult at the enterprise level where collective bargaining, constrained for many years by the central control of wages, has regained importance. But it is unlikely to flourish as it did in the early 1970s. Bargaining on wages and other "economic" conditions of work has to take into account the growing pressure of international competition; and bargaining on "qualitative" conditions is being challenged by management initiatives and new technologies which tend to frustrate collective control. Union representatives at plant level (delegates and factory councils) who have been trained mainly for "economic" negotiations, find it difficult to adjust to new objectives and strategies.

The desirability and extent of, and possible control over, decentralised bargaining is a matter of discussion and contention among the trade unions. Co-ordination between the various bargaining levels has always been weak in Italy and has been made more difficult by the trend towards decentralisation, so enlarging the scope for the informal – almost clandestine – bargaining practices traditional in Italian industrial relations.

4. The contents of collective agreements

The agenda for collective bargaining has been changing too. In the last ten years the emphasis has shifted away from wage increases towards "qualitative" issues such as job security, industrial restructuring and labour mobility. Flexibility has become a key issue in the discussions on manpower utilisation, working time and wages. While the need for greater flexibility of labour is recognised, this does not mean simply that the employer is allowed wider discretion in the use of manpower. The implementation of flexibility is subject to collective control, usually coupled with state control. Moreover, at least in intention, the goal of greater flexibility is coupled with those of promoting employment and improving the protection of existing jobs and incomes where enterprises are in economic difficulties.

In the area of working time the last two bargaining rounds have struck a compromise between the trade unions' demand for a general reduction in working time and the employers' refusal or insistence on a case-by-case approach. The employers won the argument that the issue would be more effectively handled at a decentralised level – at branch or enterprise level where a reduction in working time could be better matched with reorganisation (and flexibility) to obtain a cost-neutral result.

But the trend towards a slow reduction in general working time continues: average annual working hours in industry are down to 1,749 (38.2 hours on average per week, with an average of 36 hours in the public service).

As to wages, the most serious rigidities have been modified: the escalator clause has been slowed down and differentiated; seniority wage increments have been frozen; and the seniority allowance has been softened. Occupational wage differentials have begun to increase through collective agreements and, in part, individual bargaining, particularly in the private sector, while an increasing interest is being shown in new incentives schemes, productivity bargaining and profit-sharing. The round of enterprise bargaining, which began in autumn 1987, will probably increase the importance of productivity bargaining and result in the deferring of some wage increases to finance pensions.

A reappraisal of job-classification schemes is also under way, in order to adapt them to technological innovations.

5. The changing climate

Concertation at the macro-level has contributed to making the climate of Italian industrial relations more collaborative and less conflictual. All the indicators of conflict have been decreasing since 1976 and are now at their lowest levels in the post-war period.

A new, more collaborative climate has also emerged at the enterprise level, particularly since 1984-85. More participative and productivity-oriented labour relations have been initiated by local unions and shop stewards in an informal way, often without explicit acknowledgement by their central organisations, and accepted by individual employers. The techniques and the process are significantly different from those common in Italy's European neighbours. The experiments in participative labour relations have remained under the control of the social partners, with a minimum of formality and without any legal intervention. This marks a sharp contrast with the French and Spanish experience, which has largely been supported and regulated by legislation.

The first and most sophisticated agreements were signed in public enterprises which have traditionally played the role of "model employers". These resulted from the same process of political bargaining that has supported most aspects of Italian social and labour relations. The process of privatisation which Italian public enterprises are undergoing is similarly influenced; not only has it been politically and socially controlled but in most cases it has stopped short of depriving the public shareholders of its controlling position.

On the whole the unions have been able to reduce to a minimum their internal divisions in facing this new type of bargaining, unlike unions in Spain and France, and also in contrast with the Italian experience of central concertation. The most significant agreement of this kind, the IRI protocol, was signed in December 1984 in the midst of the battle over the escalator clause.

Flexible procedures, unity of action among trade unions and public enterprise initiatives have been three factors favouring a trade-off between participation and flexibility. Participative experiments are slowly being extended to, mainly large, private enterprises, including some of those initially inclined to an antagonistic rather than collaborative attitude towards the unions.

A contributing factor has been the provision of generous income protection for employees affected by industrial restructuring: 80 per cent of their former wage is paid by social security to employees laid off or working short time, often for indefinite periods. Such provision has made it much easier for most Italian enterprises to guarantee job security and consequently to promote a trade-off with greater internal labour mobility.

It would be simplistic to conclude that a participative and productivity-oriented pattern of bargaining has supplanted the traditional contractual practices. But the general emphasis of the industrial relations system is changing in this direction. Participation at micro-level has begun to invest concertation at macro- and meso-levels with majority support from trade unions and large enterprises – whose role in setting the tone of industrial relations is far from exhausted. The net result of this mix of multi-level participation, based on bilateral trade-offs with indirect government support, has largely been satisfactory. It has allowed Italian industry to come through the most difficult phase of restructuring with the lowest level of conflict of the post-war period, significant productivity increases and a good recovery of profitability. It has guaranteed to the trade unions relative stability in terms of membership, resources and representation within their traditional constituency, including part of the small enterprise sector. It has also favoured some trade union influence among the "cadres". Indeed, the unions received the employers' backing in including some cadres in the last bargaining round.

This experience seems to confirm the usefulness of some basic elements of industrial relations not only in periods of crisis but also in industrial adjustment – namely, a mixed degree of centralisation of the system and a practice of concertation in some way symmetric at the various levels, supported at least indirectly by government policy.

6. Perspective

More uncertain is how the Italian system will perform in the present phase of continuous innovation and uneven prosperity. Some aspects of the Italian blend of participation will have to pass a difficult test. On the union side it remains to be seen if their production-oriented commitment will last beyond the "emergency" or defensive side of industrial transformation, or will be supplanted by the traditional "distributive" approach.

Significantly, structural adjustment has been far more effective, as have policies and their results for employment, in the developed north and east of the country, where the vitality of industry can better compensate for state inertia, than in the less developed south where production-oriented tripartite co-operation is most needed. This increases the risk of widening inequalities in a country already afflicted by multiple dualism.

The distributive bias goes back to an Italian tradition of political compromise and weakness, largely sustained by a distribution of public goods which has strengthened political and social tensions. From the political arena this bias has pervaded the functioning of public administration and made it more difficult to cure inefficiency. These are probably the most serious elements of rigidity in the Italian system, and are a strong influence on the strategies and behaviour patterns pursued by the social organisations.

The tensions among political parties exert recurrent pressures on internal union affairs which are more likely to promote conflictual attitudes than to foster productivity-oriented co-operation.

Another obstacle rests with middle- and low-level officials of the unions and their organisations, who have been trained for traditional collective bargaining and show some difficulty in converting their negotiating approaches and tools to suit more productivity and service-oriented objectives.

Collective bargaining in Japan: Recent trends and problems

Tadashi Nakamura, Assistant Minister for International Affairs,
Ministry of Labour, Tokyo

1. Introduction

In 1986, 12.3 million Japanese workers (28.2 per cent of the total labour force) were members of trade unions. This represents a continuation of the declining trend in union membership, due mainly to the slow growth of employment in highly unionised manufacturing on the one hand and a rapid increase in jobs in commerce and services on the other. Since the first oil shock in 1973-74 the growth of nominal wages has slowed substantially after a period of rapid economic growth and double-digit wage increases. Unemployment is a growing concern for all parties. The unemployment rate today is close to 3 per cent, compared with about 1 per cent in the late 1960s and early 1970s. Since the yen began to appreciate strongly in autumn 1985, Japan's economic environment has become more difficult and uncertain. Management has responded by increasing efforts to adjust employment levels and reduce labour costs, while enterprises have sought new areas in which to expand their activities, including the transfer of production overseas.

Faced with these changes, trade unions have placed more emphasis than ever on job security and shortened working hours, as well as prior consultation at both enterprise and national level on the introduction of new technology and the transfer of production overseas. Tax reform has been a contentious issue between the Government (and the governing party, the Liberal Democratic Party), opposition parties and trade unions. For the Government, measures to stabilise tax revenue are seen as essential to reduce the budget deficit in the long term. Its critics have pressed for a reduction in income tax while opposing the newly introduced sales tax, particularly since wage increases are expected to be modest.

In response to the growing importance of labour issues which go well beyond the competence of enterprise level negotiation and require national policy solutions, trade unions have accelerated their long-standing drive for unification of the labour movement, which is now dominated by four rival national organisations. This initiative was scheduled to bear fruit in November 1987 when a Japanese private sector trade union confederation was to be formed as a first step towards full unification, to embrace public sector unions by 1990.

Non-intervention in industrial relations at any level is the basic attitude of the Government which essentially has two functions: the first is to provide the legal framework under which free and democratic trade unions can form and operate, and which includes a system for third-party arbitration in case of difficulties; the second is to promote dialogue between the parties concerned, including public authorities at all levels, and to help create an environment for both social partners under which industrial peace can be maintained, economic prosperity achieved, and the welfare of workers improved.

2. Wage negotiation

A series of wage negotiations (the so-called "Spring Offensive") is held each spring at enterprise level under the guidance of the national and industrial associations of employers and trade unions. This form of negotiations was first adopted in 1955 by eight industrial associations of trade unions and was later expanded to include all industries. The purpose was to enhance the bargaining power of unions against capital and to establish socially accepted levels of wage increases.

By tradition, trade unions in the metal industries, particularly steel, have led the way in wage negotiations, a position they acquired early on in the years of rapid economic growth fuelled by fast development of heavy industry and chemicals. At that time, the Government's role was to create an environment favourable for promoting constructive dialogue between the social partners and the peaceful solution of labour problems. After the 1974 negotiations, which resulted in average wage increases of 33 per cent to compensate for the sharp rise in prices caused by the oil crisis, all parties shared fears that a vicious wage-price spiral was in prospect – as had been experienced in Western developed countries. A statement by the President of the Steel Workers' Federation that the trade union would be prepared to restrain wage demands if the Government acted to curb price rises was supported by the majority of trade unions as well as by employers and the Government.

In 1975 the average wage increase was only 13 per cent. This reflected a lower rate of inflation due to effective government policies which included a freeze on public utility prices. Since then, the approach of trade unions has been to ask for wage increases which conform with economic reality. Employers, for their part, have exerted the utmost effort to modernise and rationalise production methods and organisation, with the consultation and co-operation of trade unions, so reducing labour costs as well as improving the quality of products.

Stable but slower growth in recent years has affected the Japanese economy and the general level of wage increases. Metal industries, including steel, shipbuilding and vehicles, have been most severely hit by foreign frictions and the strong appreciation of the yen. The Government has repeatedly expressed its support for the view of the Economic Council that the fruits of growth and increasing productivity should be distributed in the form of increased wages as well as shorter working hours. Trade unions in the expanding tertiary sector are expected by some to take over the lead in wage negotiations. Though nominal wages are still an important issue for negotiations in the Spring Offensive, trade unions now put more stress on real wage increases, as well as on policy issues such as price stabilisation, guaranteed employment and improvement of social security, all designed to enhance workers' real living standards.

3. Employment

Stable but slower growth, new technology, the appreciation of the yen, the transfer of production abroad, and the economic catch-up of newly industrialising countries, all imply the possibility of higher unemployment in Japan. Some estimates suggest that the appreciation of the yen alone could result in a loss of employment of 684,000. At the national level, trade union federations are demanding that the Government take action to stabilise the exchange rate, expand domestic demand, protect small and medium-sized enterprises, implement appropriate measures to tackle the adverse effects of migration of production facilities and enhance employment measures in general.

Under the lifetime employment system prevalent in Japan, workers tend to worry less about loss of their particular job, and as long as their continued employment in the same enterprise is guaranteed, they tend to be less resistant to the introduction of new technology than workers in other developed countries. Prior consultation with trade unions and intrafirm training provided by many enterprises contribute to this positive attitude of workers and unions towards technological innovation. Information technology, however, presents somewhat different challenges from those in the past, in terms of the scope and speed of its application – small-batch as well as mass production, office work as well as production lines, small as well as big enterprises.

Faced with information technology, trade unions are increasingly stressing the need for employment guarantees, education and training, industrial safety and health, and prior consultation. Many industrial federations of trade unions have adopted standards or guide-lines for the use of member unions when they are consulted by, or engage in, negotiations with the employer on the introduction of new technology. At the national level, in 1984 the Round Table Conference on Employment Policy, composed of leading figures from management, unions, universities and government agencies, reached a consensus after two years of discussion on five principles to be applied voluntarily by the parties concerned on introduction of information technology. All four major national trade union organisations referred to above are covered.

The rapid appreciation of the yen to high levels has prompted the transfer of production facilities abroad, often referred to as the "hollowing" of production. The view of business leaders is that this is essential for the survival of the enterprise and profitable for coexistence and co-prosperity in the world. At the same time, due consideration should be paid to employment security and industrial peace with the unions. But the potential levelling-off or reduction of domestic production and increase in unemployment has worried trade unions who see the transfer of production overseas as a threat. They are asking for guarantees of employment and prior consultation.

The Round Table Conference on Employment Policy has been called upon to make an in-depth study of the impact of capital outflows on the level and composition of domestic employment, with a view to arriving at a possible consensus similar to that reached in the case of information technology.

4. Working time

Total annual hours worked by the average Japanese worker have remained at 2,100 over the last decade. Though three-quarters of workers enjoy a five-day working week in some form or another, only around one-quarter have two full days off every week. In addition, only half the average 15.2 days of paid holiday entitlement are taken by workers. Generally speaking, the bigger the size of the enterprise, the shorter the scheduled working hours a week and the higher the proportion of workers enjoying a five-day working week and taking their full paid annual holiday entitlement.

Despite the fact that trade unions have recently showed a keen interest in shortened working time, this has not been reflected in the results of bargaining, partly because they still put a higher priority on wage increases when faced with a choice between the two. Instead, unions have pressed the Government to take certain measures, including the revision of the laws which stipulate maximum working time and minimum holidays, in the hope that this will help them in bargaining at the enterprise level.

Employers, for their part, see difficulties in meeting the demand of workers for shorter hours at a time of sluggish economic activity, greater competition from the NICs in both domestic and international markets, and existing wide disparities in working hours between big and small enterprises.

The Government acknowledges the importance of shortened working hours in improving the quality of working life, creating employment in the long term, harmonising working conditions with trading partners in the West and expanding domestic consumption derived from leisure. An early step was to legislate in 1985 to make 4 May a holiday when either 3 May or 5 May (which are both national holidays) fall on a Sunday, so making a "bridge" for a three-day holiday.

Several consultative bodies to the Government have stressed the need for shortened working time. In 1986 the consultative group to the Prime Minister on structural adjustment included this issue in a set of proposals for expanding domestic demand. The Economic Council set a goal of 1,800 hours a year as one of the measures contributing to structural adjustment. This level is comparable to that of the United Kingdom and the United States today, and would correspond to a uniform five-day working week and full utilisation of holidays with pay.

After long and serious discussion with trade unions and employers, the Government presented Parliament with a Bill to revise the Labour Standard Law, which was approved with amendments in the most recent extraordinary session in June 1987. The law thus revised paves the way for a maximum 40-hour week.

This will be achieved step by step by issuing government orders setting maximum working hours, with 46 hours as a starting level. The law also stipulates a minimum of ten days' paid holiday (six days before the revision) to which should be added, as before, one day for one year of employment in the same enterprise up to a maximum of 20 days. In addition, it also contains a flexibility clause in applying maximum weekly working hours which is designed to meet the needs of enterprises, particularly in tertiary industries.

5. Tax reform

The Government and LDP have taken the view that income tax should be reduced in response to a widespread feeling that the present tax burden is too heavy. However, new sources of revenue had to be found to compensate for the loss due to income tax reduction, given a persistent government budget deficit in spite of continued efforts to cut state expenditure. This has led to a re-examination of the balance between direct and indirect taxation. Japan is heavily reliant on direct taxes by comparison with other developed countries.

Opposition parties and trade unions agree that income tax should be reduced, in particular, for middle-income groups, but they have also argued that inequalities in the tax system (which is more favourable for the self-employed like medical doctors than for wage earners whose income tax is deducted directly from their pay checks) needed remedy and that, to avoid hurting low- and middle-income groups, no new indirect taxes should be introduced.

Tax reform has been a major issue of contention at every election, national or local. When prior to the general election in 1979, Prime Minister Ohira announced his intention to introduce a sales tax, his party lost many seats. At the most recent general election in 1986, Prime Minister Nakasone promised a reduction in income tax and pledged that a broadly based indirect tax would not be introduced. His party subsequently enjoyed an overwhelming majority.

The tax reform Bill presented to the regular session of Parliament in early 1987 included, among other things, a cut in income tax through reducing the number of tax brackets as well as applying progressive tax rates on income; introduction of a sales tax, though with a low maximum tax rate of 5 per cent and the exemption of food, medical care, education, and so on; and revision of preferential tax rates for workers' capital accumulation programmes and small savings (up to 3 million yen).

The reaction of opposition parties and trade unions was fiercely critical, in particular, of the introduction of the sales tax, which they claimed breached the public pledge made by the Prime Minister. Other points for dissatisfaction were: insufficient reduction of income tax; the revision of preferential tax rates for capital accumulation programmes and on small savings; and neglect of the need to remedy unequal taxation.

Opposition parties and all trade union national organisations formed a coalition to stage public campaigns against the Government's tax reform proposals. These campaigns were echoed in the mass media and even by some members of the LDP. The local elections in spring 1987, for heads of local authorities and members of local assemblies resulted in a big set-back for the LDP. All Bills related to tax reform were discarded at the end of the regular Parliamentary session in May. The new Bills presented to the extraordinary session in June excluded the clauses on sales tax and the preferential tax for capital accumulation and were approved by Parliament at the end of the session in September.

6. Unification of the labour movement

The decade after the war saw a mushroom growth of unions and their membership, with very different ideologies, approaches to trade union activities, and political allegiances. In the following decade, some moves towards unification were made by each of the four national trade union organisations but these initiatives did not bear lasting fruit, with one exception – the creation of the Japanese Council of Metalworkers' Unions (IMF-JC) as a permanent unit through which industrial associations joined IMF regardless of their affiliation with any of the national organisations.

At a later stage of the period of rapid economic growth, some trade union leaders began to express once again their concern on the need for unification of the labour movement to effectively tackle the internationalisation of the Japanese economy, changes in industrial structure, widened aspirations of union members, further improvement of workers' living standards and pluralism of the opposition parties. In some local areas, unions in the private sector created joint consultation forums independently of their affiliation with national organisations.

In 1970 the heads of the major industrial associations in the private sector formed a group to discuss common issues and, in the same year, with the approval of the four national organisations, the heads of six industrial associations started discussion on possible unification. However, this initiative ended in failure in 1972 because of conflicting views on principles, for example, whether to unify all sectors simultaneously or start with the private sector, whether to adopt an approach based on struggle or on pragmatism, whether action should be politically oriented, with the use of political strikes, or economy oriented, excluding political strikes. Following this failure, union leaders felt strongly that joint action and restoration of mutual confidence rather than discussion of principles were vital for the success of unification. In 1973 the Trade Union Conference for Joint Action was formed and in 1976 it became the Trade Union Conference for Policy Promotion. This move was reinforced by the difficulties experienced after the first oil shock when big wage increases seemed improbable and reduction and deployment of the workforce as well as restructuring of industries were inevitable. Thus the need was for action to persuade the Government to adopt appropriate policies and measures.

Parallel with the activities of the Conference, many prominent trade union leaders exerted their influence in favour of unification, though some unions in Sohyo (General Council of Trade Unions of Japan) were critical of these moves on the grounds that the Conference leaned too much to the right wing. In 1980, again with the approval of the four national organisations, the Association for the Promotion of a Unified Labour Movement was established. In 1981 it recommended that unification go ahead first in the private sector, with a programme including the need for policy-based union activities, the exclusion of dogmatic opposition groups, enhancement of ties with the International Federation of Free Trade Unions, and unification of all trade unions. Sohyo reacted to this with the reservation that the Association's opposition to the LDP should be clearly stated, there should be no discrimination in accepting unions for affiliation to the new unified grouping, and that excessive enterprise unionism should be discouraged.

The Promotion Association became the Consultative Association in 1982 with the permanent secretariat absorbing almost all the staff of the Trade Union Conference for Policy Promotion, including the President and Secretary-General. The basic conception has been further refined. In November 1987 the Japanese Private Sector Trade Union Confederation was to be established with Mr. Tateyama (Churitsuroren – Federation of Independent Unions of Japan) as the President and Mr. Yamada (Domei – Japanese Confederation of Labour) as the Secretary-General. The Confederation will encompass 54 industrial associations with a membership of 5 million. It hopes to achieve unification of all trade unions, including those in the public sector, before 1990.

Labour and economic indicators

Year	Economic growth rate[1] (%)	Labour force (1,000 persons)	Unemployed (1,000 persons)	Unemployment rate (%)	Employed (1,000 persons)	Employed in tertiary sector (1,000 persons)	Rate of wage increase[1] (%) Nominal	Rate of wage increase[1] (%) Real	Average yearly hours worked
1955		41 940	1 050	2.5	17 780	8 110			2 338
1965	9.8	47 870	570	1.2	28 760	13 450	8.1	4.1	2 315
1975	7.8 17.0[2]	53 230	1 000	1.9	36 460	20 690	16.8 15.8[2]	8.2 9.1[2]	2 064
1985	4.3	59 630	1 560	2.6	43 130	25 850	6.22	1.6	2 130
1986	2.5	60 200	1 670	2.8	43 790	26 070	3.5	3.1	2 102

[1] Yearly rate is computed from the average of the last ten years. [2] Computed from the average of the period 1965 to 1973.

Number of union members

Year	Total	Sohyo	Domei	Churitsuroren	Shinsanbetsu	Others
1955	6 286 [35.6]	3 094	237	34		
1965	10 147 [34.8]	4 250 (1 670)	1 658 (1 549)	961 (961)	61 (61)	3 218 (2 945)
1975	12 590 [34.4]	4 573 (1 635)	2 266 (2 106)	1 369 (1 368)	70 (70)	4 705 (4 395)
1985	12 418 [28.9]	4 339 (1 699)	2 154 (2 012)	1 549 (1 548)	60 (57)	4 785 (4 552)
1986	12 343 [28.2]	4 268 (1 682)	2 126 (1 986)	1 601 (1 600)	61 (59)	4 784 (4 555)

Notes: [ ]: Estimated organisation rate. ( ): Number of union members in private sector. SOHYO: General Council of Trade Unions of Japan. DOMEI: Japanese Confederation of Labour. CHURITSUROREN: Federation of Independent Unions of Japan. SHINSANBETSU: National Federation of Industrial Organisations.
Source: Ministry of Labour: *Basic survey of trade unions*.

Collective bargaining in the Netherlands: Recent trends and problems

Mr. H.J. Brouwer and Mrs. L. Kootstra, Ministry of Social Affairs and Employment,

in co-operation with

Mr. J.K. Bout and Mr. J.W. Van Den Braak, General Association of Employers, Netherlands Employers' Federation

1. The economic context

For both internal and external reasons, the Dutch economy was marked by falling employment in the late 1970s and early 1980s. Together with a sharp rise in the labour supply this led to a steep rise in unemployment from 7.5 per cent in 1980 to 17 per cent in 1983.

Slowing economic growth and rising unemployment resulted in a substantial increase in social security expenditure. Together with falling revenue from natural gas, this produced a very large government deficit (which rose from 3 per cent in 1973 to 10 per cent in 1983) and a strong increase in the burden of taxes and social security premiums (from 46 per cent in 1973 to 53 per cent in 1983).

Adjustments to social security schemes and economies in government spending became inevitable. Control of wage costs became equally necessary.

Since 1983, real progress has been made in the reduction of the government deficit and securing some decrease in social security contributions. However, the reductions that had been planned have not yet been achieved.

Fortunately, since 1984 there has been a marked improvement in the employment situation, thanks to the restraint in wage costs and growth in world trade which is so essential to the Netherlands. Unemployment, though, is still at an unacceptably high level (around 14 per cent in 1987, against 3.5 per cent in 1973) and among the unemployed there is a growing hard core of long-term jobless.

For this reason an active, more targeted labour market policy is indispensable, alongside a balanced general economic policy. Such a policy mix will only be effective if the Government and social partners accept joint responsibility for it and make a concerted effort. Tripartite as well as bipartite consultations at national level, and collective bargaining in branches of industry and enterprises, have an essential role to play. Before going into more detail about the relationship between economic development and policy and collective bargaining, it is worth making a few remarks about the relations between the Government and the social partners in the 1970s. This background information is necessary to make recent developments clearer.

In the 1970s, rapid increases in wage costs contributed to the decrease in employment in the private sector. Moreover, there was a strong link by law between the actual trend in wages in industry on the one hand and the annual increase in social security benefits on the other. A similar firm, almost incontestable, link also existed between wages in the private sector and salaries in the public sector. This provided a major incentive for the Government and politicians to interfere directly with the formation of wages in the private sector. For a number of years there was a standard pattern of failed talks between the social partners, resulting in the Government taking legislative measures to try to control wage-cost increases.

2. Changes in the relationship between the social partners and the Government

The Dutch model of harmony, with a long-standing tradition, became one of confrontation and polarisation. This situation was no longer tenable, either for the social partners or for the Government.

In the 1980s Dutch industrial relations are not as highly centralised as they were. Bipartite discussions between the social partners have become more important. Discussions between the social partners and the Government have come to be focused increasingly on co-ordinating respective policies.

A milestone in this development was the November 1982 agreement between the social partners in the bipartite Foundation of Labour. The agreement provided a general framework for pursuing policies aiming at a moderate wage trend which would make for an improvement in profits, as well as a redistribution of employment among more workers. With this in mind, the Government did not implement a wage freeze as it had intended, but relied on the social partners to regulate matters for themselves.

The agreement has set the trend for industrial relations to date. In 1984 the agreement was extended by recommendations on youth unemployment. In 1986 the agreement was updated with the goal – endorsed by the Government – of reducing unemployment substantially (by 30 per cent) between 1986 and 1990.

The Government itself has implemented significant policy changes in the 1980s. One of the first things that had to happen, partly because of the necessity to make adjustments in the social security field, was a severing of the strong links which existed in the Netherlands between wage development in the private sector and the trend in civil service salaries and social security benefits. A more independent policy came to be conducted in the public sector, though developments in the private sector were not entirely disregarded. Wage restraint in the private sector continued to be a matter of great urgency both for economic reasons and also to prevent over-large divergencies between the better-off and the less well-off. But the basic difference from the preceding period was that the iron link between collective bargaining and the trend in social security benefits had been severed.

3. Changes in the wage formation process

This adjustment of public sector income determination illustrates the significant turn in the Dutch wage formation process. More attention came to be paid to the independent position of the social partners as regards wage negotiations. The Government's decisive role in controlling the process came to be considered as less and less fruitful. Increasingly, two major drawbacks to frequent government interference were felt. First of all, the prospects of possible government intervention disturbed the negotiating process between employers and unions. Negotiations were either pre-empted before they could start, because the scope for wage increases had already been laid down in legislation, or the bargaining position of employers was weakened by the realisation that if wage costs were really to get out of hand, government action would restore the balance. Secondly, frequent government interference proved to be a major obstacle to decentralised wage bargaining. The need for decentralised wage bargaining became urgent when negotiations ceased to be predominantly focused on percentage wage increases. More complicated packages, including reductions in working time and measures making for greater flexibility, required specific solutions at sectoral and enterprise level. In addition, the decentralisation of wage negotiations will make it possible to adapt wages more closely to sectoral increases in productivity and hence to continue the overall moderation of real wage increases.

Wage restraint in the Netherlands has led to an auspicious trend in labour costs and export prices in industry and is thus of vital importance to employment. The Government, employers and trade unions still share this point of view. Recently, talks have been held between the Government and the social partners on this subject. The main item of discussion has been how to continue wage and employment policy along the lines of the earlier agreements within the Foundation of Labour.

4. Changes in collective bargaining

In the meantime there has been a major development in the negotiating process between the social partners. Though there is still some central co-ordination, among employers as well as among unions, more freedom has been created for differentiation in (decentralised) negotiations in branches of industry. From 1982 onwards negotiations have been very much influenced by the unemployment situation, in line with the agreements referred to.

The first collective agreements after the agreements at national level have followed a rather similar pattern in most sectors of the economy. In the majority accord was reached on a general reduction in the wage trend (no pay increases to compensate for rises in the cost of living), making possible a reduction in working hours of 5 per cent from an average of 40 to 38 hours a week.

In the last two or three years the results of bargaining between contracting partners in the private sector have shown more varied patterns. Greater attention has been paid to specific circumstances in each sector; profitability and the labour market situation have particularly affected the negotiating results. More attention has been paid to the training of employees. To improve the position of the unemployed, the Government is increasingly supporting training programmes in which the unemployed can participate.

In actual bargaining on collective agreements greater attention is expected to be given to improving the labour market position of the long-term unemployed and unemployed young people. Such measures will be supported by government policy to help these groups. Under certain specific conditions employers may be exempt from paying employers' social security contributions for a period of two years if they take on long-term unemployed persons. This measure has been developed in tripartite discussions. For young unemployed persons the Government will introduce a youth work-guarantee scheme. On a temporary basis additional jobs will be created in the public and semi-public sector to guarantee work experience for all unemployed youngsters. Once the work-guarantee scheme comes into force young people will in fact receive wages, work experience and training instead of receiving social security.

5. Away from regulating wages

Up to 1982 wage policy was based on rather detailed and powerful legislation. With the 1982 agreement a new phase began – no longer direct interference by the Government but independent responsibility and freedom for the social partners.

To illustrate this avenue away from legislation, the Wages and Salaries Act of 1970 has recently been changed. Government interference in the wage formation process is restricted to emergency situations arising from sudden shocks to the national economy coming from abroad.

At the end of 1986 the Act on wages and salaries for non-collective agreement employees expired. The Government has decided on further liberalisation in this field. Wages and salaries for this category of employees are no longer restricted by law.

To give another example of deregulation and liberalisation in the wage formation process, up to 1986 there was tight control by the Government on wages in the semi-public sector (health, welfare, public transport and the like), under pressure of severe budgetary constraints from the late 1970s onwards. However, this policy threatened the bargaining freedom of employers and unions, especially in the semi-public sector. For this reason the Government sought a new balance between its own responsibility on the one hand and the responsibility of employers and unions in the semi-public sector on the other. In January 1986 the result was permanent legislation to allow for freedom of bargaining in the semi-public sector. The Government, responsible for financing semi-public services, sets aside a budget for the cost of collective agreements financed by taxes on social premiums. Employers and unions take full responsibility for the contents and implementation of the collective agreements. Since the legislation was introduced in 1986, several collective agreements have been brought about without any need for intervention.

6. Final remarks

In conclusion, three points are worthy of emphasis. First, Dutch industrial relations are characterised by a common responsibility for the fight against unemployment.

Second, the wage formation process has been considerably liberalised in the Netherlands. Since 1982 it has been generally accepted that wage formation is the responsibility of the social partners themselves. Instead of direct intervention in the process of wage formation the efforts of the Government will be directed at lowering the burden of taxes and social premiums which are still relatively high in the Netherlands.

Third, both sides of industry and the Government are convinced that wage moderation and specific labour market measures must go side by side. Incomes policy is no longer a goal in itself but has become instrumental in labour and employment policy.

The competitive position of the Netherlands in international markets has improved. Wage costs have been moderated. More and more specific measures on unemployment policy are being agreed to in the negotiations on collective agreements. It is necessary to continue on this course.

Collective bargaining in New Zealand: Recent trends and problems

Mr. Bob Hill, Director, Employment Policy, Department of Labour

1. The context

Over the last three years the New Zealand Government has implemented a number of liberalisation measures designed to encourage greater efficiency and productivity throughout the economy. These have included floating the New Zealand dollar, removing interest rate controls, removing agricultural support measures, progressively dismantling trade barriers and undertaking a series of taxation reforms. In addition to this, the Government has pursued contractionary monetary and fiscal policies in an effort to stabilise the economy.

Despite the short-term impact of the stabilisation and liberalisation measures undertaken by the Government, the level of economic activity, as measured by real GDP, increased in both the years ended March 1986 and 1987.

This growth, though, has not been distributed evenly. While the urban economies of Wellington and Auckland, and the service sector, have remained relatively strong, most non-metropolitan regional economies and the primary and manufacturing sectors have come under pressure.

Overall, employment growth at first slowed, and then became negative, with registered unemployment rising sharply to 91,667 in September 1987, representing 6.9 per cent of the labour force. Unemployment is concentrated among the young, the non-European and women. Unemployment rates are higher outside the main centres, and particularly outside Wellington and Auckland.

Unlike previous periods, when employment fell and unemployment rose, the number of people taking up new jobs or leaving old ones has remained at historically high levels. This suggests that the decrease in employment and increase in unemployment is primarily related to structural changes in the wider economy.

It is within this economic context that this report analyses recent trends in collective bargaining in the private sector only in New Zealand. Collective bargaining in the state sector will be subject to substantial change in the next year, with the intention of aligning state mechanisms, practices and procedures with those that exist in the private sector.

In order to understand trends and developments in collective bargaining in New Zealand it is also necessary to have some understanding of the history of the institutions that until recently have dominated the industrial relations system. The system, which has recently been reformed by the Labour Relations Act, was founded on compulsory conciliation and arbitration in order to eliminate strikes and lock-outs and to create a process that equitably distributed the fruits of production. The main features of the system were therefore:

- union registration whereby a union was recognised as the sole legitimate representative of a group of workers;
- compulsory conciliation and arbitration which fixed wages and conditions of employment. A central feature was the determination of awards which extended wages and conditions across an entire industry or occupation;
- enforcement of awards by the Department of Labour, which turned to the Arbitration Court for enforcement actions.

For more than 70 years, this system of third-party intervention, which was paramount in wage fixing, was overseen by the Arbitration Court. The Court evolved two main approaches to wage fixing. These were:

- the fair wage, which involved extending the wage that a good employer paid across an entire industry. Firms that could not pay this rate ceased production;
- the living wage, which involved an assessment of the wage necessary to sustain a man, his wife and two children.

The primacy of the Arbitration Court began to wane and was ended by the "nil wage order" in 1968. The interventionist role shifted to the Government under the guise of wage controls. The living wage and the fair wage were transformed into regular cost-of-living adjustments to maintain base-line purchasing power in real terms.

Under the pressures of economic stagnation, the idea of promoting equity through wages came to be increasingly questioned because:

- the growth in unemployment highlighted the need for wages to reflect more precisely the supply and demand for labour;
- the model of the family as a man (earning a wage), his wife, and two children ceased in many cases to represent the actuality;
- the growth in the welfare state focused attention on the social wage as an important element in determining the well-being of people.

The Government now intends that wages should be fixed by free collective bargaining between employers and unions. Gone is the emphasis on compulsory arbitration and on third-party intervention.

There are four major features of the Labour Relations Act that reflect the rise of free collective bargaining and the decline of compulsory conciliation and arbitration. They are:

- endeavouring to break the dependence of trade unions on the State. This is done through measures designed to promote amalgamation or restructuring of unions, e.g. a requirement for minimum union membership of 1,000, easing the ability to amalgamate, and competitive union coverage;
- continuing with voluntary arbitration in wage fixing, which was established in 1984;
- binding, in a more contractual sense, employers and unions into either an award or an agreement by constraining the scope for negotiations during the term of the award or agreement. This is reinforced by a clear definition of when a strike or

lock-out is unlawful (or lawful) and by providing substantial sanctions against unlawful actions;
- requiring unions and employers to enforce their own awards and agreements and to meet negotiation costs.

2. The repercussions of economic, technological and social developments on workers' organisations

Returns made to the Registrar of Unions have indicated that membership has remained relatively static over the past few years. Unions, however, have pressed strongly for the reintroduction of compulsory unionism which would ensure that "freeloading" by non-union members would not occur. This happened in 1985, after more than a year of voluntary unionism, in the form of post-entry closed shops where this is agreed to by employers or a majority of a union's potential membership.

Membership will also have been affected by the decline in primary and secondary industries, traditionally well organised, and the growth in the service sector, where union penetration is weaker. Research has shown that in 1981, 74.7 per cent of manual workers were unionised compared with only 55.1 per cent of white-collar workers. One response to this trend has been the formation of the Council of Trade Unions, uniting unions belonging to the Federation of Labour (the central body for private sector unions), the Combined State Unions and non-affiliated unions such as the Bank Officers, Insurance Workers and Local Bodies Officers, within one organisation. The intention is to establish a body that can provide co-ordinated and comprehensive leadership for the trade union movement in its dealings with both governmental and employer interests.

Unions have tended to be organised on an occupational basis for historical reasons, as common interest was originally along occupational lines. Some unions cover occupations which are fairly industry-specific (e.g. seamen, woollen mill-workers), whereas others have members scattered through numerous industries (e.g. drivers, clerical workers). Again for mainly historical and geographical reasons, most unions are small, with approximately two-thirds of all registered unions having less than 1,000 members.

Changes to union registration have been made in the Labour Relations Act in order to strengthen union structures and to provide greater opportunities for union coverage to change. These have stemmed from the Government's commitment to a strong trade union movement, resistant to the declines that have affected their counterparts in the United States and the United Kingdom, for instance. First, unions will require 1,000 members for registration, which will permit the resulting larger unions to benefit from economies of scale in terms of servicing their membership.

Secondly, previous constraints on amalgamation have been dropped to allow amalgamation wherever union members consider they have a community of interest with other union members. Considerable consolidation in union structures is already resulting from these moves.

Thirdly, new unions will be able to be formed wherever workers are not already covered by an award or agreement, despite notional coverage by any other union. In addition, where workers are dissatisfied with their own union's performance and/or where another registered union believes it can offer a better service to those workers, procedures exist for that union to extend its coverage after separate ballots of all the groups of workers concerned. Despite the existence of "non-poaching" agreements it is expected that the procedures will result in considerable changes in union coverage over time.

Trade union reform is underpinned by provisions in the Act which require unions to provide fully for democratic membership participation and for accountable management structures. The result may be unions which are larger, better funded, more efficient and somewhat more responsive to their members' needs. It is expected that the total number of unions will drop from 230 to less than 100 within the next two years.

3. The role of the State in industrial relations

The leading role the State has played in industrial relations has already been highlighted. In addition to the statutory framework in which the industrial relations system operates, general wage controls existed in the period under review right up until 1984. They were lifted for a period in 1977 but in 1979 a policy of selective intervention was introduced. This was aimed at influencing the level of settlement of the early trend-setting awards and ensuring that "break outs" did not occur as the wage round proceeded. Then moves towards the concept of tripartism were adopted, again providing the back-drop against which the Government could influence wage levels. Finally, a total freeze on wages was imposed from 1982-84. The wage freeze was removed by the present Government after tripartite talks resulting in an agreement on reform of the wage-fixing system.

One result of previous interventions was the further development of a network of rigid relativities between bench-mark positions in different occupations, which transmitted the increases in trend-setting awards to other awards and agreements. Some of these relativities were, in fact, established in response to the wage controls so as to justify wage increases. Another result was the compression of margins for skill when flat-rate rather than percentage wage increases were regulated for. To limit the importance of historical relativities and to ensure that settlements would be determined more by the supply of and demand for labour, arbitration was made voluntary in 1984 and the criteria used by the Arbitration Court were related more to economic factors than to those of historical relativities.

Another constraint on free collective bargaining which has been removed by the Labour Relations Act was the limitation of matters that could be negotiated into a registered award or agreement to "industrial matters". Thus, there are now no restrictions on the scope of negotiations, and bargaining on subjects as diverse as the introduction of new technology, superannuation schemes and the provision of child-care facilities can occur.

In essence, the Government's policy for collective bargaining is that the State should have no role in direct negotiations between unions and employers. This is reflected in its commitment not to intervene to determine the outcome of industrial disputes. Its formal input is now limited to the Tripartite Wage Conference, where representatives of the Government, employers and unions meet in advance of the annual wage round. This Conference now serves largely as an information-sharing exercise, with the Government outlining for the other parties the economic environment within which they will be responsible for negotiating their respective awards and agreements.

Unions and women's groups are currently campaigning for the introduction of legislation to enforce "equal pay for work of equal value" on the basis of skill, effort, responsibility and working conditions. In spite of the Equal Pay Act, 1972, women in New Zealand earn, on average, 78 per cent of men's average hourly earnings. "Equal pay for work of equal value" could also be achieved through collective bargaining. However, employers are generally opposed to the notion of "equal pay for work of equal value", arguing that supply and demand factors should be paramount in wage fixing.

At present, a government-commissioned *Equal pay study* is reviewing the Equal Pay Act, 1972 and will make recommendations as to the necessity of legislative changes to that Act.

The Government is also reviewing the operation of its recently introduced voluntary code on occupational health and safety, although again no decisions have yet been taken to introduce any legislation.

4. The structure of collective bargaining

At the core of the industrial relations system has been the negotiation of awards with "blanket coverage", also known as "extension". The principles behind this system have been that:

(a) the award provided a common minimum rate for a particular job across all employers in an industry. In so doing it:
   - constrained the extent to which competition between workers for jobs could drive down wages; and
   - equalised the labour costs for employers across an industry: competition between employers was therefore based on factors other than labour costs.

(b) the award provided the means by which the fruits of production could be distributed to the greatest number of workers via the bargaining process;

(c) award negotiations simultaneously resolved a large number of disputes.

Awards provided for minimum rates only. Individuals could be paid above these rates and unions could also negotiate "second-tier" agreements above award rates.

The Labour Relations Act established the principle that each worker should be covered by only one settlement which is comprehensive in nature. Depending on the choice of the union, this may be either an award (where blanket coverage may be negotiated) or an agreement which the union makes on behalf of its members. Such awards and agreements are binding on the parties once settled and "second-tier" bargains cannot be enforced unless they are composite awards or agreements, where common settlement is reached between several unions and an employer(s). This exception is made in order to limit the number of negotiations any one employer may be involved in. For instance, there may be workers represented by 20 different unions in some plants. All parties are keen to see the development of more composite bargaining.

The future of national occupational awards is more controversial. Deregulation in the economy has highlighted the differing economic performances between firms, between industries and between regions, and this is difficult to reflect in such awards. However, many unions are committed to retaining the award structure and many employers prefer negotiations to take place on such a basis, as it limits both their and their employees' direct involvement. On the other hand, many employers strongly advocate the development of decentralised bargaining at the workplace level.

While there has been little reform to date, there are encouraging signs that some occupational awards will in future be negotiated on an industry-by-industry basis, for instance, and that composite bargaining at the workplace level will be much more widely used.

5. The substance of collective bargaining

As highlighted in section 3, the maintenance of rigid historical relativities are of great concern. Despite the existence of voluntary arbitration since 1984, these relativities have by and large been maintained by the traditional method, i.e. the pattern for the wage round is effectively set by a handful of key awards which are negotiated early in the piece, leaving little scope for negotiation in those that follow. Change here is very much dependent on changes in the structure of bargaining, and there has been insufficient time since the passage of the Labour Relations Act to assess whether structures more relevant to industries and individual workplaces will develop.

In general, real wage costs to industry have been reduced over the past few years. This has largely reflected workers' concerns over job stability and the inability of employers to pass increased costs on easily in a less regulated economy. Unfortunately, the extent to which moderate wage settlements have tended to produce higher levels of employment by limiting the costs of employing labour has not been determinable. The high level of structural adjustment taking place, where wage moderation in itself may not be sufficient to preserve employment, has not made it easy to persuade unions that such moderation is either desirable or effective. Where job losses do become inevitable, however, there are no longer any legislative constraints on redundancy agreements that may be negotiated.

Other forms of labour market flexibility have not been the subject of a great deal of agreement to change by the parties to date, although there have been some moves towards more flexible working arrangements, including greater provision for shift work and the greater use of part-time employees. No significant campaign has been directed towards a reduction in working hours, however. Questions of the introduction of new technology had been the prerogative of management under previous legislation, although union involvement in the process was often accepted. Now that bargaining is not limited to "industrial matters", matters such as this may be the subject of negotiation. Over time this may lead to a more widespread range of issues being addressed.

6. The climate of collective bargaining: Disputes, co-operation and participation

As with the substance of collective bargaining, the recent introduction of free collective bargaining makes it difficult to assess the climate in which it will operate, as the structures are still very much in the early stages of development. The present framework, being permissive, will allow the development of both co-operative and adversarial approaches to bargaining. Both of these approaches are present in any system of industrial relations, where workers and employers are both greatly affected by the relative success or failure of an enterprise, but where the returns to that enterprise must be divided in some way.

Recent trends in days of work lost to strikes and lock-outs have been highly variable. In the first six months of 1986 a record total of 1,125,864 working days were lost. Most of these days were lost as a result of a prolonged strike in the meat export industry, in which significant structural adjustment is taking place, while the effect of moving out of the wage freeze continued to be a contributory factor. Over the same period in 1987 only 81,677 working days were lost. This reflected in part the Government's policy of non-intervention in collective bargaining and disputes, resulting in agreements more likely to be adhered to and regulated by the parties themselves, as well as the impact of recession in many areas of the economy. These recent trends provide little assistance in assessing likely future trends. While the emphasis in the Labour Relations Act on greater sanctity of agreement should result in much less "wildcat" and unlawful industrial action, strikes and lock-outs that do occur are likely to be over substantial issues affecting large numbers of workers.

There is little evidence to show that industrial democracy is widespread in any form outside the confines of collective bargaining. The Government intends therefore to investigate ways in which to promote industrial democracy in the workforce.

7. Conclusion

Free collective bargaining between employers and unions has existed in New Zealand for only a very short period. Whether the permissive provisions contained in the Labour Relations Act will lead to the negotiation of awards and agreements that are relevant to the industry or workplace in which they apply will depend largely on the attitudes of employers and unions. To the extent that unions ignore the need for wages to be more closely related to productivity and the differing positions of workers in different firms, industries and regions, and employers remain reticent to share information and to accept that their own workers and their respective unions have a legitimate role to play in their enterprises, flexible and relevant settlements will be limited in number. Such a situation would ensure the maintenance of a slow adjusting, low-wage, low-productivity labour market and hence an underperforming economy. It is to be hoped, however, that both parties will exercise their largely unfettered powers of collective bargaining wisely.

Bargaining systems, incomes policies and conflict in the Nordic countries

Professor Nils Elvander, the Swedish Council for Management and Work Life Issues

1. Introduction

The Nordic countries provide a very rewarding field for comparative societal research, particulaly in the area known as industrial relations. On the one hand certain fundamental features of their political and economic systems coincide, and all four countries are equally homogenous as regards cultural patterns and religion. In many other countries these factors provide grounds for party political or trade union groupings, but not in the North. On the other hand there are certain fundamental differences as regards the rules for solving conflicts, the forms of incomes policy, and the State's role as the direct or indirect employer in the public sector. These divergencies stem mainly from the different experiences of the four countries since the emergence of industrialism, modern trade union systems, and political democracy. Historical factors also explain most of the differences in organisational structure, particularly in trade union structure, which can still be seen today, even though the economic, social and political systems of these countries have grown increasingly alike. The historically determined nature of this union structure in turn affects rule systems, incomes policy, and the public employer function. I shall give some examples of this below, both country by country and in a comparative perspective.

Industrialisation reached Denmark as early as the 1870s, i.e. much earlier than in Norway, Sweden or Finland. This has two important consequences which help to explain the distinctive nature of Denmark's organisational structure, its rule system and so on. First, modern rules and institutions for conflict solution evolved earlier here than in the other countries, and it evolved to an unusually high degree under the auspices of the parties actually involved. For example a basic agreement was reached between LO (the Danish Trade Union Confederation) and DA (the Danish Employers' Confederation) in 1899, whereas the first such agreement was not made in Norway or Sweden until the 1930s, or in Finland until the 1940s. Secondly, the organisational structure in Denmark was long imbued with a persistent small-industry guild tradition, with the result that the principle of the large industrial union has not yet been adopted in the DA-LO area, and the solidarity of LO and FTF (the National Association of Danish Unions of Salaried Employees) is rather weak. This fragmented organisational structure is probably the main reason why the mediation system has been given such far-reaching powers and why government intervention has been so common, even in connection with incomes policy agreements during the 1960s and 1970s. It should be added here that, despite the different union structure, DA has none the less always enjoyed more or less the same strong formal powers as its counterparts in Norway and Sweden as regards approving national union agreements and lock-out decisions. AFC (the Finnish Employers' Confederation) on the other hand, did not acquire corresponding powers until the 1950s.

The union structure is even more fragmented in Norway, where union membership also amounts to about 60 per cent as against 80 per cent in the rest of the North. LO has retained much of its centralised power structure since the beginning of the century, but the effect of this is partly offset by a strong tradition of direct democracy whereby decisions regarding agreements and mediation proposals are decided by a ballot of the members. Such ballots are also common in Denmark and in some areas of the trade union movement in Finland. In Sweden advisory ballots have been held, but not since the centralisation of LO during the 1940s and 1950s. In Norway direct democracy is strong even in the white-collar unions which reveal a far more fragmented pattern than their equivalents in the neighbouring countries. There is still no real equivalent in Norway to the Swedish TCO (the Central Organisation of Salaried Employees). The strength of the ballot tradition and the fragmented union structure together explain the strong position of the mediation system in Norway and Denmark, whereby the National Mediator has powers to combine different agreement areas in a single vote on mediation proposals, and they also help to explain the exceptional importance of compulsory arbitration in Norway. It seems to be a general rule that the more direct democracy there is, and the greater the anarchy prevailing in the union system, the greater is the need for "dictator solutions" by arbitration or direct government intervention.

Sweden emerges as the direct opposite of Norway and Denmark as regards trade union structure and the freedom of the labour market from state intervention. Representative democracy is paramount in the trade union movement, and for most of the period since the war and until the 1980s, the unions have been more centralised that they are in the other three countries. The forces of centralism have been so strong in Sweden, partly because large-scale industry emerged here at an early stage and has enjoyed a strong position, and because a strong Social Democratic Party governed the country almost interruptedly for 44 years in close collaboration with large-scale industry. The strength of the organisational system is the main reason why freedom on the labour market has been so consistently and successfully upheld, compared with the situation in the other Nordic countries. The unions and the employers reject any suggestion of strengthening the loosely organised mediation system. There has only been one case in which compulsory government intervention has actually been imposed in a labour market conflict – the 1971 conflict involving SACO/SR (the Central Organisation of Swedish Professional Organisations). Protection against "socially dangerous" conflicts in the public sector is determined by the parties themselves, although since 1965 the Swedish public employees have had the most extensive rights to strike and to bargain of any country in the world (in itself a sign of union strength). There is no government apparatus for incomes policy as in the other Nordic countries; incomes policy is regarded as a dirty word, although even in Sweden the practice has in fact been not uncommon during the 1970s and 1980s.

Finland occupies an intermediate position between the Danish-Norwegian model with a fragmented trade union system and extensive state intervention in conflict situations on the one hand, and the Swedish model with its strong centralised unions and the rejection of government intervention on the other. Finland has the same pattern of union organisation as Sweden – particularly in the white-collar sector which is also represented by one large central union, TOC (the Central Organisation of Salaried Employees), and one smaller academic union – and a fairly similar rule system for conflict situation, although the National Mediator has slightly wider powers than the temporary mediation commissions in Sweden. But there is an element of political fragmentation in the Finnish trade union movement that has no equivalent in the other Nordic countries, namely the strong standing of the communists in FFC (the Finnish equivalent of LO). The fact that as many as one-third of all FFC members still support communist policies can be seen as a legacy of the civil war and of the repression of communism during the inter-war years. It should also be remembered that the transition from an agrarian to an industrial society, and the accompanying introduction of modern industrial relations, did not occur in Finland until after the Second World War. The political split in the trade union movement has led to a higher rate of conflict than in the other Nordic countries, and also goes a long way towards explaining why, since the start in 1967-68, the State has participated more frequently and more actively in general incomes policy solutions than is the case in the other Nordic countries.

My aim in this short comparative survey has been to demonstrate the power of tradition. To a great extent the actors on the labour market are the prisoners of structures and rule systems generated long ago. It would be just as difficult to envisage the Norwegian system without compulsory arbitration as it would be to envisage the introduction of compulsory arbitration in Sweden. But this does not mean that everything is fixed irredeemably in the old paths, nor that the actors lack all freedom to introduce successive changes into the present structures and rule systems, within the basic framework of the existing order. In fact quite big changes appear to be under way in all four countries. Let us examine the winds of change that are now blowing over the North.

2. Bargaining systems – a period of transition

In all four countries, as in the rest of Western Europe, decentralisation of the bargaining system seems to be the order of the day. The trend is most evident in the private sector, but appears to be spreading into the public sector as well. In Sweden this development is very noticeable at the present time, and seems to have its counterpart in the other Nordic countries. The questions addressed below are all connected with this. But first, let us look back at developments since the end of the 1960s, the period covered by the reports.

In Denmark, ever since the 1930s, LO and DA have been making two-year central agreements according to a previously ratified "schedule", after which the rest of the labour market follows on, taking their soundings from the DA-LO agreement. During the 1970s the centralised bargaining system began to come under heavy pressure as a result of the stagflation crisis: a major conflict in 1973 and compulsory solutions imposed by legislation in 1975, 1977 and 1979. Intervention on the part of the State, which generally took the form of mediation proposals being made mandatory by law, was always undertaken by Social Democratic governments in combination with incomes policy measures. This led to conflicts between the Government and LO, and within LO support began to emerge for a decentralisation of the bargaining system. The 1981 pay talks were decentralised and proceeded smoothly. The 1983 talks were also largely decentralised but operated within an overall frame of 4 per cent per year, introduced by the new non-socialist government and combined with the abolition of the traditional compensation for inflation. In 1985 LO tried to force through a central agreement, but after a major conflict the Government intervened, introducing legislation to prolong all agreements within the extremely narrow overall frame of 2 per cent per year. In 1987 the pay talks were once again fully decentralised, and resulted in four-year agreements on the pattern of the metalworkers' agreement.

Like Denmark, Norway has a tradition of central two-year agreements between LO and NAF (the Norwegian Employers' Confederation), which also provide a "signpost" for the rest of the labour market. On a few previous occasions, for instance in 1974, bargaining had been conducted at the national union level, but since 1982 this seems to have been the rule. Co-ordination has sometimes been extended to include tripartite incomes policy agreements, most recently in 1976 and 1980. As in Denmark, the Government has often intervened in the talks, generally by calling for compulsory arbitration. This was the case both in the LO-NAF area and elsewhere. In 1978-79 a compulsory price – and wage freeze – was imposed, and in 1981 there was an unsuccessful attempt to limit wage drift by law (which in Norway runs at the record level of two-thirds of the total wage increase as against one-third to one-half in the neighbouring countries). This year all parties have agreed to abstain from wage increases during the second year of the current two-year period. NAF appears to have an ambivalent attitude towards the arrangements for bargaining. As in Denmark, support for decentralisation has grown most vigorously *within LO*. This is probably because of the problem of the many maverick groups outside LO, which often show little sign of social responsibility. In particular there is a clutch of new unions in the sometimes extremely inflationary oil sector.

From 1956 to 1981 there were co-ordinated pay talks between SAF and LO in Sweden. As a rule the central agreements, for periods of varying length but usually for one year, were also followed by the other parts of the labour market. But sometimes the private white-collar workers (since 1974 included in the private white-collar workers' cartel, PTK) and the power and the powerful organisations of the public sector have been in the vanguard and have acted as wage leaders. To a greater extent than their counterparts in the other three countries, SAF and LO seem to have lost their position as the pivot and central source of norms for the bargaining system. This is mainly because a growing schism between the public and private employees has been having a disabling effect on LO ever since the major conflict of 1980. But it is probably also due to the fact that the changeover to a decentralised system at the beginning of the 1980s was launched by SAF against LO's will – which represents a fundamental difference in comparison with Denmark and Norway. It was SAF who insisted on centralised bargaining in the 1950s, but it was VF (the Engineering Employers' Association, the leading member association in SAF) which signalled the break in 1983 by making a separate agreement with the metalworkers' union. The following year bargaining at the national union level operated without any co-ordination in the SAF-LO area and under strong competition from the public sector, which led to agreements in breach of the Government's inflation estimates. This in turn led to various government interventions, all smacking of incomes policy. In line with the Government's stated wishes, low-level frame agreements, including wage drift, were reached. In 1985 the agreements were for one year, and in 1986 for two years for the whole labour market.

In Finland during the 1970s and 1980s central bargaining has generally been conducted in the private sector, and since the first so-called Liinamaa agreement in 1968 it has been a question of broad incomes policy agreements incorporating a substantial element of social policy. During the 1980s this co-ordination with incomes policy has been under heavy pressure, and major groups both inside and outside FFC have either threatened to strike or actually done so in order to achieve central agreements or to force through changes in the agreements. Pay talks have sometimes been conducted on a national union basis (1980, 1983) and sometimes centrally (1981, 1984, 1986). The national union agreements were for a year, while the central agreements covered two-year periods. As in Sweden, the employers are raising the demand for decentralisation while FFC is trying to resist the pressure, partly out of consideration for the co-ordination with incomes policy. For a long time the authority of the FFC leadership in relation to the unions seems to have been much weaker than the LO leadership's relations with its unions have become over the last few years in Sweden. The labour movement seems to have as much difficulty as its counterparts in Sweden and Norway in asserting itself against the increasingly powerful white-collar and academic groups. The central incomes policy agreements are threatened by intensive rivalry between the trade unions, and by the resistance of the employers, and sometimes also by the failure of the Government in recent years to fulfil its part of the tripartite agreements.

In the light of this comparative survey, several questions arise which can perhaps provide material for a discussion.

(a) How far can decentralisation be pushed? Is it possible to decentralise bargaining to the corporate level (something which to my knowledge has not been seriously suggested in the Nordic countries)?

(b) How can we solve the conflict of interest which seems to obtain in the employer camp as well as on the union side between *(a)* the desire to curb the rate of wage increases, e.g. by central frame agreements, and *(b)* the need for local freedom of action which can generate a certain wage differentiation and adjustment to market conditions?

(c) Is it possible that an alternation between central agreements on general issues such as general wage limits, working hours, and the equalisation of sickness benefits (e.g. the two-year agreement in Sweden between SAF and LO in 1986) on the one hand, and agreements at the national union level on the other, could solve the problem of satisfying overall long-term interests as well as specific national union demands?

(d) How far can the public sector adapt itself to the private sector, as regards the decentralisation of bargaining and a certain differentiation in wage formation?

3. The problems of incomes policy

In discussing incomes policy problems I shall not report on the separate countries, partly because the main lines of development have already been indicated in the previous section on bargaining systems. Instead I shall focus on some general features of the related problems, and shall illustrate these with examples from the different countries.

The first question is connected with the political conditions for an incomes policy. Given the current definition of incomes policy – i.e. government action associated directly or indirectly with collective bargaining and aimed at curbing wage increases – it appears that this policy represents one link in a government's economic policy as a whole. The government thus becomes directly or indirectly a third party in the bargaining process. Consequently there arises a certain conflict with the cherished right to free bargaining, regardless of whether the element of incomes policy-making is temporary or permanent (no permanent incomes policy approach has been adopted in the Nordic countries, except possibly between 1968 and 1972 in Finland). Naturally the tension between incomes policy and free bargaining will be aggravated whether incomes policy is combined with a conflict resolution imposed by law, as was the case in Denmark during the 1970s. This highlights the whole question of the political conditions of incomes policy. The Danish LO could only accept state intervention of this kind – and even then unwillingly – when it was imposed by a Social Democratic government, but when a non-socialist government intervened in he same way in 1985 LO opposed it. In fact, according to LO, a real incomes policy which gives wage earners something in exchange for the curb on free negotiations can only be carried out by Social Democratic governments.

It is a common belief that an effective incomes policy can only be conducted by a government that enjoys the confidence of the wage-earner associations, i.e. in practice, a Social Democratic government or one in which Social Democrats predominate. The experience of the Nordic countries seems to confirm this idea, despite occasional examples of non-socialist governments conducting an effective incomes policy that reduces the rate of wage increases (i.e. in Denmark). To the Danish examples already quoted can be added the "comprehensive solution" of 1963, which was also the product of a Social Democratic government. The first incomes policy package agreements in Finland at the end of the 1960s were introduced by the so-called People's Front Government, which included communists – one of the main reasons, it is thought, why they were a relative success. Every government since has included Social Democrats. Since 1982 the Social Derncocratic Government in Sweden has been conducting a *de facto* incomes policy, which perhaps might not have been possible under a non-socialist government; it has included selective changes in tax rates, price freezes and the funding of corporate profits, informal agreements on general limits and – last but not least – extremely tough action in the role of public employer in the 1986 pay talks. Norway's experience suggests something of the same pattern: the Social Democratic government tried to introduce an incomes policy, while the non-socialist government which took over in 1981 abstained from doing so. The Danish Government's tough approach since 1982 could be called an incomes policy, but it has not been combined with the customary barter with the unions.

This *de facto* connection between incomes policy and Social Democratic government raises some important questions of principle:

(a) How can an effective and reasonably long-term incomes policy be combined with the parliamentary principle of shifts in power? If not a permanent, at least a continuing, incomes policy may be needed to achieve balance in the national economy. But does not this presuppose a "Finnish" system of coalition governments which include Social Democrats?

(b) Can an incomes policy be conducted by a Social Democratic government if it is opposed by white-collar unions of no particular party affiliation? This problem has recently come up in Sweden, where during the 1980s TCO has on occasion protested against incomes policy trends. But the question seems to be becoming general, and to be acquiring greater import as the white-collar groups continue to expand.

(c) An incomes policy which is based mainly on agreements between LO and a Social Democratic government (or a coalition government with Social Democratic participation) is very much at risk from splinter groups inside or outside LO. We can see examples of this in Denmark during the 1970s and in Finland over the last few years. Regardless of the political composition of the government, any incomes policy type of restraint will come up against the free-rider problem, and the risk that members will lose confidence in their unions is great. But these difficulties are probably aggravated when the incomes policy is conducted under the auspices, as it were, of the labour movement itself. Is it possible to avoid a situation in which an ambitious "Social Democratic" incomes policy ultimately weakens the central union organisations on whose participation it depends?

In conclusion a few questions can be raised about the effectiveness of the various tools of incomes policy.

(a) Will not fiscal policy (consisting mainly of reductions in marginal taxation) soon have exhausted its role as an object of barter with the unions? Since the Haga Agreements of the early 1970s, the Swedish experience has been that any form of link between fiscal policies and pay talks has simply served to complicate rather than facilitate the talks and has not generally led to the desired restraint in wage demands. Moreover, the need as well as the opportunity for fiscal bartering would disappear if the Nordic countries were to follow the international trend in fiscal policy, i.e. largely eliminating the marginal taxation problem, extending the taxation base, and substantially reducing the opportunities for high income earners and capitalists to make deductions and go in for tax planning.

(b) Can price freezes, the funding of corporate profits, restrictions on share issues and other measures aimed at the corporate sector ever be anything more than a symbolic political gesture, when in fact it is in the interests of the government (regardless of its political colour) and of the unions that companies should be competitive and their investment opportunities good?

(c) In what circumstances can the general limits laid down by the government on wage cost increases be effective? Can Sweden's 1986 model – allowing for estimated wage drift in the central agreements and adjusting for "surplus drift" at the end of the contract period – provide a general solution to the problem?

(d) Can the public employer function represent an effective instrument of incomes policy? Experience in Sweden over the last few years suggests that this is almost the only weapon in the incomes policy arsenal which has not been exhausted. The Government and the public employers used it in the combative 1986 bargaining rounds – among other things they succeeded in throwing out the automatic adjustment to wage developments in the private sector – and the Minister of Finance is now talking in terms of cash limits on public wage costs. Can the Government simply use its employer role to impose a desired level of wage cost increases on the labour market as a whole?

4. Conflict and conflict resolution in the public sector

In all four Nordic countries the public employees represent a significant, and until the 1980s, a rapidly growing sector of the labour market. In Denmark, Norway and Sweden their share of the labour force is about one-third while in Finland it is a little less. In all the countries the public employee unions have acquired more power and independence since the great expansion of the public sector began during the 1960s, and their demands for adjustment to wage developments in the private sector – in other words compensation for wage drift – has been a great and constant source of conflict. This demand, which is often formulated in terms of solidarity with the low income earners and adjustment to the market in the case of the highly paid academics, has become the most powerful cause of conflict. During the 1980s the curb on growth in the public sector in the Nordic countries has led – as in most Western countries – to a rise in the number of conflicts. Every legal conflict in Sweden since the great conflict of 1980 has been fought in the public sector; and even in 1980 the four large unions of the public employees – the white-collar cartels TCO-S and KTK and the two LO unions for the state employees and the municipal workers, popularly known as the "Gang of Four" – played a notably active part.

But these structural similarities between the Nordic countries should not conceal the fact that there are also fundamental differences, particularly when it comes to the scope of the right to strike and the rules for conflict resolution. These differences have historical roots. The earlier evolution of democracy meant that workers and the lower ranks of the white-collar sector in Denmark and Norway achieved full rights to bargain and strike before their counterparts in Sweden and Finland. On the other hand the "continental" administrative tradition in Denmark and Norway still prevents the higher ranking public servants from enjoying the right to strike (particularly in Denmark). When the full right to negoiate was introduced in

Sweden in 1965 and in Finland in 1970, the tradition of independent administrative departments meant that the right was extended more liberally to the public sector. Adaptation to the rules of the private sector has advanced furthest in Sweden, with Finland in second place. Denmark – where over 100,000 higher public servants have no right to strike – has gone neither as far nor as consistently as the other three countries when it comes to replacing a public by a private law approach.

The rule systems for solving conflicts concur with those that evolved on the private labour market, and are thus also historically conditioned. In Denmark and Norway the State can intervene by legislation or by compulsory arbitration. In Sweden and Finland special committees representing the parties involved are set up to examine whether a particular conflict constitutes a public danger, but they cannot settle a dispute on the issue with binding effect. In Finland, these committees have a neutral chairman (the National Mediator), but this is not so in Sweden – which confirms that the mediation system has a stronger position in Finland than in Sweden.

Regardless of the compass of the right to strike and the way the rule system works, conflicts in the public sector appear to have increased in both number and scope in all the Nordic countries over the last decade. Perhaps this means that making changes in formal rule systems is not the best way of securing peace on the public labour market and avoiding conflicts that are a public danger. Furthermore, the rule systems are deeply entrenched in history and are thus difficult to change in any fundamental way. The unions achieved the right to strike after a long struggle and they are not likely to abandon it willingly. A better way might be to introduce certain constraints, such as arrangements in basic agreements for ways of protecting particularly sensitive areas of the community, for example the caring sector, the legal system and defence.

We may also ask ourselves whether the difference between the public and private sectors is still as great as people usually say when it comes to the relative strength of the parties involved, the effects on third parties, and the question of public danger. Are not retrenchments and recruitment freezes beginning to undermine job security also in the public sector? Is not the saving that accrues to the public employers from unpaid wages during strikes outweighed by the damage to public opinion, particularly when they answer a strike with a lock-out? Sweden's experience in 1986 suggests that the battle for public sympathy can determine the outcome of a conflict: the State and municipal employers, who were co-operating exceptionally closely, decided to respond to a doctors' strike in the spring by imposing a lock-out on teachers, which proved extremely unpopular. Subsequently they revised their strategy and refrained from using the lock-out weapon when the "Gang of Four" struck in October; this time public opinion went against the strikers (except the nurses, who had everybody's sympathy). And finally: cannot conflicts in the private sector also hit third parties and become a public danger? As modern societies are developing the two sectors are becoming increasingly intertwined and interdependent, which tends to iron out any difference between them as regards the societal effects of conflict.

The best solution to the growing frequency of conflict in the public sector would probably be to find suitable ways of guaranteeing equality in wage trends, which all parties in principle agree to. Up to now the weakness of this kind of guarantee clause seems to have been that the private employees have perceived them as unjust, mainly because their rigidly automatic design makes it difficult or impossible to introduce even *desirable* wage differentials and because they imply that even "justified" productivity-related wage drift calls for compensatory adjustments. The automatic compensation for wage drift often means that wage differentials between public and private employees for which there is no real justification are simply confirmed. If the basic principle underlying the solidaristic wage policy – equal wages for equal work, regardless of where people are employed – is to be feasible, the demands of the public employees for compensation must not obstruct changes either upwards or downwards in wage differentials. Perhaps the answer could be the solution which emerged as one of the chief consequences of the major public sector conflict in Sweden in 1986: namely, the automatic element in the wage drift guarantee was dropped, and the whole question of possible compensation for any declared lag in relation to the private employees during the period of the agreement was postponed until the 1988 pay talks as an unresolved issue of conflicting interests. In other words, the parties may negotiate and dispute about possible compensation in the next bargaining, but there is no guarantee that such compensation will be the same for everybody, as it has been in the past.

Collective bargaining in Norway: Recent trends and problems

Mr. Knut Groholt, Director-General, Ministry of Local Government and Labour, Oslo

1. The context

The problems and challenges facing workers' and employers' organisations in Norway, as in other industrialised countries, have changed greatly in the course of the last ten to 15 years. As a result of developments in the world economy and in technology, considerable changes have taken place in the overall conditions to which the Government and the labour organisations in Norway must relate. The demand for readjustment has increased both in tempo and extent, and it must be assumed that this development will continue. Change has become constant.

2. The repercussions of economic, technological and social developments on workers' and employers' organisations

In the space of only a few years significant changes in the structure of industry have taken place in Norway. There has been greater emphasis on service industries than on manufacturing industries, and the public sector has grown. The transition from an industrial to a service-related society can be illustrated by tables 1 and 2, showing these sectors' relative proportion of employment and added value (GNP) in three selected years, 1974, 1980 and 1986. The figures relate only to mainland Norway.

Just under 60 per cent of the working population in Norway belong to a workers' organisation. The proportion of organised workers has remained at more or less the same level for the past 25 years, and seems to be quite stable.

Nevertheless, developments in trade and industry have had a considerable influence on the activities of workers' and employees' organisations. The proportion of traditional industrial employees is diminishing, while that of white-collar workers is increasing. This is due to the above-mentioned structural changes involving

Table 1. Employment by sector as a proportion of total employment (in percentages)[1]

Sector	1974	1980	1986
Industry and mining	25.33	22.28	19.54
Service sector	34.70	36.35	39.63
Public administration	19.35	22.54	23.99

[1] Excluding shipping and petroleum activities.

Table 2. Added value by sector as a proportion of GNP (in percentages)[1]

Sector	1974	1980	1986
Industry and mining	24.27	19.98	18.11
Service sector	42.92	45.56	46.10
Public administration	14.43	17.04	16.87

[1] Excluding shipping and petroleum activities.

transition from traditional industry to the service sector and growth in the public sector. The relative proportion of white-collar workers in traditional industry has also increased.

The dominant workers' organisation is the LO (Norwegian Federation of Trade Unions), which has about 770,000 members of whom 150,000 are pensioners. The YS (Confederation of Professional Unions) also has a broad membership, but its main recruiting ground is among lower and middle-ranking white-collar workers. It has approximately 122,000 working members. The AF (Federation of Norwegian Professional Associations) has some 127,000 working members and consists primarily of professionally based organisations for university and college graduates. Workers' organisations that do not belong to the LO, YS or AF cover about 170,000 employees, the biggest of them being the Norwegian Union of Teachers and the Norwegian Nurses' Association.

Developments have led to increased competition between these organisations. Although the LO is still the dominant employees' organisation its share of unionised employees has fallen. In 1958 the LO's share was 84.7 per cent but by 1983 this had fallen to 64.1 per cent.

The trends in union membership among workers can be illustrated by the overview given in table 3 for the years 1958 and 1983. The figures do not include pensioners.

The organisational structure among employers in the private sector is dominated by the NAF (Norwegian Employers' Confederation), which is a collective organisation representing a number of industry associations and companies having direct membership. In all the NAF has around 10,000 members, with approximately 370,000 employees. The employers' organisations in trade, banking and insurance are not members of the NAF.

The Government is an employer with approximately 180,000 employees and conducts separate negotiations with the employees' organisations. The municipalities are employers with approximately 260,000 employees and conduct central negotiations via the Norwegian Associations of Local Authorities.

Changes in occupational structure and educational level will have direct and indirect effects on organisational structure and on the way in which employees move between organisations. Both the changes in membership and the increased competition to attract members are placing new demands on the organisations.

Table 3. Trends in union membership

Membership	1958		1983	
	No.	%	No.	%
LO	501 875	47.5	612 263	35.8
Other organisations	90 730	8.6	342 076	20.0
Non-union	463 395	43.9	755 661	44.2

Naturally enough it is the large central organisations, for workers and employers, with their broad range of members, that are experiencing these demands most acutely. Groups that have traditionally set the pace have found their proportion of the total membership falling. At the same time new groups are increasing their relative importance, so that the centre of gravity in the central organisations is shifting. The changes in the composition of the working population are creating a demand for changes in the structure of the organisations. In order to strengthen their position five of the major industrial unions in the LO have decided to merge into one large industrial union. One of the main purposes of this move is to create an organisation better adapted to the changed structure of employment, by means of which there will be improved opportunities to recruit the new groups of workers.

In this connection the organisations face difficult challenges. It is important to their future strength that they succeed in tackling the underlying conflicts of interest in a satisfactory manner.

Another factor which, along with the structural changes, will affect the organisations and the process of wage settlement, is the question of wage relativities and of which sectors are to lead the way on wage levels. Those who work in industries vulnerable to competition have been dissatisfied with the fact that in recent years parts of sheltered industries have set the pace on wages. On the other hand, certain groups in the public sector assert that their relative position has worsened in relation to comparable groups in the private sector. The organisations in the public sector have therefore demanded that this negative relative wage trend be reversed.

Throughout the years wage negotiations have been dominated by only a few large organisations. These have developed into powerful and influential institutions. In recent years some smaller independent organisations have been established. There is a trend in the direction of steadily increasing specialisation in occupations and division of labour markets that has provided the basis for the emergence of a more fragmented organisational structure. Some new organisations have achieved influence far beyond that indicated by their size. This applies to key personnel who, due to their central positions in the work organisation, have been able to exert considerable bargaining power. In this connection we might mention workers on oil installations in the North Sea. It is difficult to be certain as to what consequences this will have in the long term. However, there is reason to presume that the increase in the number of participants may affect the bipartite and tripartite co-operation carried out by the organisations.

Within the new occupational groups there are many who choose not to be organised in a trade union. This is especially true in connection with new companies in high technology industries which must be presumed to be growth sectors in the years to come. The employers' organisations in this case are meeting the same problems as the trade union movement. Only to a minor degree have they managed to incorporate the new high technology companies in their ranks. For this reason it is important both for the trade unions and the employers' organisations to find out why these groups do not regard joining an organisation as being in their interests.

3. The role of the State in industrial relations

The labour organisations and the Norwegian authorities co-operate constructively in several fields. The organisations take initiatives and have advisory functions both in matters relating to labour law and politico-economic affairs.

Since there is a close connection between general economic policy on the one hand and development of wage costs, prices and competitiveness on the other, the authorities place great emphasis on an open dialogue with the organisations on these issues. Permanent bodies have been established where representatives of the Government and the organisations meet regularly, where the economic situation is discussed and where the authorities submit their views on incomes policy.

In Norway wage settlement is left to the employers' and employees' organisations, and the authorities do not wish to interfere in these negotiations. However, the authorities strive to facilitate them. Since 1916 there has been a permanent mediation institution in existence to which the organisations are referred for help before a conflict breaks out if negotiations between the parties involved have reached a deadlock, the mediation institution must be notified formally that the negotiations have failed. The parties also have to submit to compulsory mediation before industrial action is taken. In recent years there has been a considerable increase in the use of the mediation institution, with 60 cases of mediation in 1978 and 123 in 1986.

In addition, a permanent committee, the Technical Calculation Committee for Wage Settlements, prepares annual overviews of trends in wages, prices, competitiveness, and so on. The members of this committee comprise representatives of the authorities and the national organisations for employers and employees. The committee's reports constitute important background material for the parties involved in the wage negotiations.

Although wage settlement is the responsibility of the negotiating parties, from time to time the authorities have made contributions which either directly or indirectly are part of the settlement, or which have a more indirect effect by forming part of the basis on which the parties judge demands and offers. In the 1970s the State participated actively in several wage settlements by going in as a third party and offering to implement tax reductions, for example. In such cases, the State's action "replaced" part of the traditional wage increase. This form of intervention has however now been abandoned, and in the present decade the State has played a more subdued role.

Reliable background material, exchange of information and discussion continue to be a natural and central part of "the Norwegian system". However, today any economic contribution made by the State in connection with wage settlements takes a more indirect form. In this connection, employment policy immediately springs to mind. All the political parties in Norway agree that maintaining a high employment rate or "full" employment is a prime goal. Thus maintenance of full employment has been a central objective of economic policy in recent years. Perhaps the State's most important contribution to incomes policy has been the allocation of significant resources to employment schemes.

The State also has the possibility of using its role as a leading employer to implement incomes policy, for example reducing the rate of price rises by curbing nominal wage increases in the government sector. Another goal may be to reduce the growth in public sector budgets. As an employer the State can also try to change the profile of wages in the public sector.

Since the authorities basically have no part to play in sorting out wage matters or revisions, it is important that the organisations should be aware of their responsibility, and that they should have an overall policy in which the public interest is allotted the appropriate weight. If this prerequisite is lacking it will be difficult for a system involving free right of negotiation to function in a modern society with manufacturing and service industries.

The existence of large organisations, which represent broad groups of employees, increases the probability that there will be sufficient regard for society's needs. They are more willing to look at employment, competitiveness and other factors in context, and they are more inclined to take into account the consequences their policies on wages will have for socio-economic conditions and employment.

The ILO's instruments also reflect this viewpoint. Its protection of the freedom to organise is first and foremost related to the most representative organisations. In this connection it is important to note that the number of small organisations that do not belong to a national organisation has increased. For small organisations representing special groups it is not as natural or straightforward to have regard for the overall public interest. Because of their key positions in certain sectors small organisations have obtained considerable influence. This may have an effect on the bargaining system. In the short run special groups can cause unrest and imbalance by outstripping what are regarded as justifiable wage limits in socio-economic terms. In the long run this may have negative consequences for the major organisations, in that their authority in the eyes of their own members is weakened and they may lose members.

In this situation the question of what role the small organisations should play poses a dilemma. In Norway the social partners are extremely occupied by this issue, and we would urge the ILO to make a special assessment of the role of small organisations in relation to the bargaining system.

4. The structure of collective bargaining

Collective bargaining takes place at a large number of levels. It is typical of Norway that there are a number of national agreements within the individual industry branches, and many branch organisations are members of a collective organisation. This structure provides a basis for two forms of settlement that differ in principle, namely individual union settlements and co-ordinated settlements.

The co-ordinated settlements used to dominate. However, in recent years there has been greater interest in union settlements, and all the national settlements in the 1980s (1982, 1984 and 1986) have been of this kind. Nevertheless, it must be emphasised that both forms of settlement are central settlements, albeit to different degrees.

Wage settlement in Norway takes place traditionally by means of a combination of central and local bargaining. Access to local bargaining and its importance vary considerably between agreement areas. Any negotiations at the level of individual undertakings are conducted during the period of the central agreement, and increases that are given in such cases are regarded as wage drift.

In the central revisions of the wage agreements a considerable amount of work is put in by the organisations, and the settlements are regarded with great interest by employees, employers and the authorities. However, it is a matter for concern that the increases agreed at the central level have gradually come to constitute a smaller part of total wage growth throughout the year.

In the course of the 1980s in certain sectors, negotiations at the level of the individual undertaking have acquired increasing economic significance. In some parts of the private sector increases that are given locally during the agreement period have become the most important to employees. Wage drift various from year to year, but in recent years it has constituted around 80 per cent of annual wages growth in the private sector. In other sectors, for example in the public sector, local bargaining has had a minimal impact. It must be emphasised that within private industry, too, there are significant differences regarding access to local bargaining and its importance.

Figure 1 shows how wage rises in selected years from 1970 to 1985 have been split between increases linked to central wage settlements and wage drift for workers in companies organised in the NAF. This group has been chosen because there is satisfactory statistical material, but it should be emphasised that other groups in industry also experience significant wage drift.

Local wage settlement is based in principle on companies' ability to pay and their demand for labour or desire to retain their employees. Today there is an increasing tendency for the market to determine wage settlement. Labour that is in particular demand is offered especially favourable terms. In this respect the market mechanism controls wage development more tightly than previously. However, at the same time the local negotiations are affected by the fact that employees will often compare themselves with employees in other companies whether or not these are in the same sector.

It might well be thought that wide variations in wage drift would result in greater differentiation of wages. However, this does not appear to be the case. It must be

Figure 1. Composition of wage increases for employees covered by the NAF

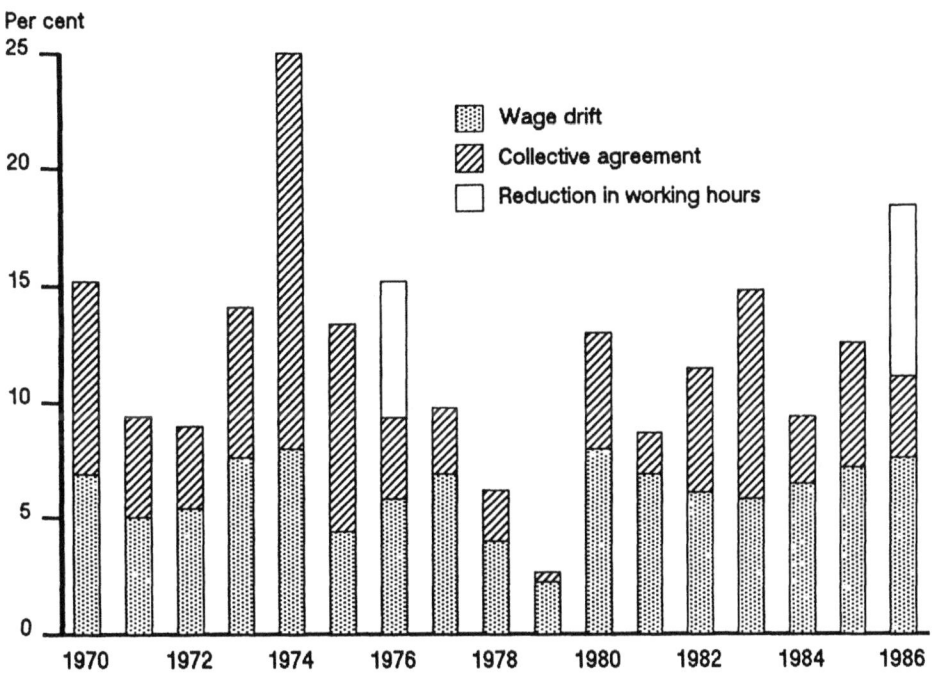

Source: NAF: Lonns- og fravarsstatistikk 1 (Kvartal, 1980 and 1987).

presumed that the reason is to be found in the importance attached by employees to preserving their relative position on the wage scale in relation to other groups of employees they use for comparison. If wage drift has a strong effect on wage differentials there will be demands for larger central increases by groups gaining little from wage drift and wanting to regain previous relative positions. For this reason it is possible that the manner in which central and local bargaining in Norway has been combined up to now has itself contributed to increasing nominal wages growth.

The growing importance of decentralised company-level bargaining is affecting both the employees' and employers' organisations. The big employees' organisations have found that their influence on incomes settlement is waning. The employers' organisations are concerned about the pressure on wage levels that accompanies large local increases. If the big organisations are to increase their influence on wage settlement, one possibility would be to determine central frameworks that embraced local increases.

The tendency towards increased use of local bargaining could also reduce the ability of the authorities to implement an effective incomes policy. Some of the classic instruments presuppose that the central organisations have the ability to commit their members to pursuing defined objectives of incomes policy. This is difficult to achieve in a system where most wage settlement takes place locally.

5. The substance of collective bargaining

Co-operation in the labour sector embraces a broad range of subjects. Several different co-operation procedures are used, the substance of which may partly overlap. In addition to collective bargaining Norway has a well-developed system aimed at giving employees a share of influence at work. Employees have the right to participate in the administrative organs of the company through co-operative bodies in the company and by means of organisational changes that give the individual employee greater influence over his or her own work situation.

Collective agreements in Norway normally consist of two parts. One is the general framework agreement which mainly regulates collective organisational questions, such as representation, co-operation, treatment of disputes and rules governing agreements between the parties. This part is called the Basic Agreement. The Basic Agreement between the LO and the NAF, which was concluded in 1935 and is often called the Labour Charter, has set the pattern here. Today there are a number of basic agreements for the various settlement areas. The Basic Agreement between the LO and NAF is valid for three years, and no industrial action is permitted during its revision.

The second part of the collective agreement mainly regulates wages and working conditions. It normally has a duration of two years, with the possibility of renegotiation of wage matters after one year. When such agreements are under revision the ban on industrial action is only applicable until compulsory mediation has been carried out.

The diagram opposite illustrates the stages in the settlement of a collective agreement:

Naturally enough wage questions dominate the collective negotiations, but many different issues form the subject of bargaining between employers' and employees' organisations in Norway.

Among other things there is a long tradition of negotiations concerning working hours. For example, in connection with the collective settlement in 1986, negotiations in the LO/NAF area led to a reduction in the working week to 37.5 hours for everyone. When the collective agreements are revised in 1988 the question of a lower retirement age will be an important subject. Any reduction in the retirement age would require close co-operation between the authorities and the employers' and employees' organisations.

Collective bargaining does not merely encompass matters linked to the individual employee's contractual conditions. Organisation of work and introduction of new technology are matters that strongly occupy both the trade union movement and employers. The LO and NAF have concluded a framework agreement concerning technological development and computer-based systems. The purpose of the agreement is to ensure that employees, through their elected representatives, receive information and the right to participate in connection with the introduction of new technology.

Further, a supplementary agreement to the Basic Agreement has been concluded which concerns development of work organisation in companies. In accordance with this agreement the LO and NAF, along with associated organisations,

Figure 2. Stages in the settlement of a collective agreement

        Negotiations
        Termination of agreements
        Exchange of demands
        Opening of negotiations

Failure of result of negotiations. Collective termination of jobs (Basic Agreement, section 20). Notification to State Mediator (Labour Disputes Act, Art. 28,31).	Negotiations result in agreement. Proposed new agreement adopted by voting, and new collective agreement is signed.

        Mediation (Labour Disputes Act, Art. 27-29)

Mediation fails to produce solution or proposal for new agreement is rejected by voting. Labour dispute (strike or lock-out) may take place four days after mediation has ended or four days after proposal has been rejected.	Proposal for new agreement is submitted and adopted by voting. New collective agreement is signed.

commit themselves to supporting and encouraging developmental work in individual companies. A number of projects and development schemes have been implemented around the country. As examples of other areas of long-standing co-operation one might mention productivity and the working environment, introduction of new technology, workplace design, administrative and planning systems, as well as improvement of the quality of products and services.

  Moreover, the State and the employers' and employees' organisations have now reached agreement on the joint financing and development of a centre whose purposes will be to develop more democratic forms of company organisation. The objective is, by means of a programme aimed at developing expertise in the labour sector, to create better workplaces and at the same time better companies. Expectations concerning the results of this work are high.

6. The climate of collective bargaining: Disputes, co-operation and participation

In conclusion, it is important to emphasise that a cordial atmosphere exists between employers' and employees' organisations in Norway. This does not mean that there are no situations where strikes or lock-outs are implemented. As late as the collective settlement in 1986, the NAF imposed a lock-out affecting some 100,000 employees. However, this major labour conflict did not have lasting after-effects. One indication of this might be that in concluding this year's collective wage settlements the employers' and employees' organisations did not have to resort to mediation before agreeing that no central wage increase should be given. Thus, in spite of disagreements regarding the solution of specific problems, the employers' and employees' organisations in Norway have arrived at a mode of co-operation which can be used fruitfully to solve labour problems.

Collective bargaining in the United Kingdom: Recent trends and problems

Mrs. Ann Mackie, OBE, FIPM, Employee Relations Adviser,
Unilever UKCR Ltd., London

1. The context

In the early 1980s, the economy of the United Kingdom suffered a far more severe recession than other industrialised economies, due to a number of factors including an overvalued currency and a substantial number of firms which had lost ground in terms of international competitiveness over many years. Unemployment climbed to over 15 per cent as businesses adjusted to the new market situations. However, the economy has now recovered, with manufacturing output climbing above the 1979 level, while growth across the economy as a whole has averaged 3.1 per cent. Similarly, inflation is under control, unemployment has been falling and productivity has been improving rapidly.

To keep pace with international competition, industry in the United Kingdom has had to adapt its work processes, often accompanied by the introduction of new technologies. This has had repercussions for the structure and organisation of work, as traditional demarcations between different categories of employees have been broken down.

The structural change experienced by the United Kingdom during the 1980s is most dramatically typified by the decline in employment in manufacturing industry. The effects of this on collective bargaining have been considerable. Traditionally, the manufacturing sector has been heavily unionised, with a high degree of trade union membership among manual employees in particular and recognition of trade unions for collective bargaining being widespread. This pattern has also been changed by the rise of the service sector, where work structure and the level of unionisation are markedly different.

The composition of the labour force has also changed considerably. Part-time employees have increased as a proportion of employees in employment and now account for 24 per cent of the total. The main area of concentration of part-time employees has continued to be the private non-manufacturing and public sectors. In the manufacturing sector, there has been a decline in the proportion of part-time employees, which can be largely accounted for by the structural changes within that sector.

There has also been an increase, in recent years, in the use of other flexible employment arrangements. These have taken two major forms: casual temporary employees used when demand requires them, and outside contract employees brought in to undertake specific jobs or tasks. Research suggests that such arrangements have been used more extensively in the private sector, than in the public sector, being particularly common in manufacturing industry, with a positive correlation between the level of capacity utilisation and the use of such "non-core" employees. The indications are that firms operating at or near full capacity were more likely to use them, than those operating below this level, illustrating that companies see them as means to match employment and output levels.

2. The repercussions of economic, technological and social developments on workers' and employers' organisations

During the 1970s there was a considerable growth in union membership amongst white-collar employees, female employees and public sector employees. This contributed to the steady growth in union membership, which in 1979 reached a peak of 13.4 million members. However, in the 1980s, this trend has been reversed, and union membership has declined markedly, largely because of the structural changes that have occurred within the economy. The closure or contraction of many large-scale manufacturing plants, where union membership was formerly very high, has been a major factor behind the overall decline in numbers.

As suggested earlier, there have been changes in the structure of the labour force, which in turn has caused changes in the structure of union membership. Part-time and other "non-core" employees have not been as easy for unions to recruit and the areas of expanding employment have been those with relatively little tradition of trade union membership and recognition.

At the same time there have been a number of significant changes made in the 1980s to the laws affecting trade unions. Acts passed in 1980 and 1982 removed some of the immunities trade unions previously held and reduced the ability of trade unions to negotiate and enforce "closed shop" agreements, requiring employees to be trade union members as a condition of employment. The 1984 Act aimed to make unions more accountable to their members, by making strike action possible only with majority support by the members. Further changes to increase the accountability of trade unions to their members will be made in the near future.

In response to the changes outlined above, certain unions have made moves to modernise their organisation, internal structures and activities. The signs are that other trade unions are now starting to undertake similar reviews.

Membership of employers' organisations has remained fairly constant, but their role has evolved to meet the changing circumstances of the 1980s. Their involvement in collective bargaining has on the whole reduced, though in many sectors it remains important. A prime growth area for them has been their role in advisory work and the provision of services to members, as well as their traditional representative functions. They are now able to offer member companies professional advice and information on a far wider range of subjects and a variety of services, including for example managing industry-wide pension arrangements. It is this ability to adapt which has enabled them to remain important institutions within the economy.

3. The structure of collective bargaining

When commenting on collective bargaining in the United Kingdom it is necessary to distinguish between the private and public sectors. In the public sector the major characteristic is that of centralised national bargaining, with large groups of employees (e.g. health service employees, the police force, civil servants) all receiving nationally agreed settlements. There have been some moves away from this, with the Government being keen to encourage decentralisation of pay determination, as illustrated by the recent Teachers' Pay and Conditions Act, which includes provision for different pay awards to be made in different areas of the country. However, there still remains a considerable uniformity within this sector, hence the rest of the discussion will concentrate on the private sector.

Collective bargaining remains a very important feature of pay determination in private sector manufacturing, with 70 per cent of plants being covered by a collective agreement. Collective bargaining is much less widespread in the non-manufacturing sector and among white-collar employees as a whole. However, the structure of collective bargaining is rather complex and a distinction needs to be made between "multi-employer" and "single-employer" bargaining. The former has undergone a secular decline which started in the 1960s, as the tight labour markets allowed the shop-floor to be more influential in pay bargaining, and which has paradoxically continued in the very different conditions of the 1980s as individual firms have attempted to match their settlements with their own economic outlook.

One must, however, go even further than this simple "multi-/single-employer" distinction, and consider how different issues can be negotiated at different levels, in the form of multi-tier deals. The trend has been towards a decentralisation in negotiations concerning pay, combined with some centralisation of negotiations concerning other conditions, such as holidays and weekly hours. Thus in many sectors there is an involvement for companies at both levels.

Amongst small firms, industry-wide deals are of particular significance providing them with a bench-mark for determining their own pay levels. National agreements also provide them with guidance on such aspects as disputes procedures, hours of work and holiday entitlement.

Within large firms, there has been a trend in at least some instances towards greater decentralisation of bargaining to the plant level, allowing individual business units to match their pay awards to their own performance. A further development of importance has been the reform of the Wages Council system, which sets statutory minimum pay rates for some 2.75 million in such sectors as retailing, hotels, catering and clothing manufacture. Under legislation introduced last year, these are now restricted to setting a single minimum rate and a single overtime rate. They can no longer determine grade rates above the minimum or other conditions of service.

One final factor that should be noted is the existence of a large number of workers who are not covered by any sort of collective agreement.

4. The substance of collective bargaining

The concept of labour flexibility has been widely discussed in the 1980s. It is seen to have benefits both to the individual firm by relating employees' numbers and work patterns more closely to its needs, so strengthening its competitive position, and to the economy as a whole by reducing rigidities within the labour market. Flexibility is a wide-ranging subject and can therefore feature in many ways in collective bargaining. However, for simplicity it can be considered in essentially three different forms, namely flexibility of work function (i.e. employees carrying out a wider range of work), time (the use of flexible work patterns) and numbers (use of "core" and "peripheral" workers to vary the size of the workforce).

On flexibility of function, the 1980s have seen many agreements which have broken down old demarcations between jobs, and at the same time equipped employees with the skills to undertake a number of tasks. Much attention has been paid to the "multi-skilling" of manual workers in the manufacturing sector, but the more flexible use of employees has been a general feature of firms as a whole. Such changes have been accepted by employees for a variety of reasons, including the recessionary conditions, the improved job security produced by such arrangements, the improved rewards often attached and increased job satisfaction.

Flexible working time agreements can take many forms, ranging from the introduction of shift-working right through to the use of "annual hours" (i.e. the setting of a total number of hours to be worked in a 12-month period by a variety of patterns). The need to use capital equipment more intensively, given the economic conditions, has led to the acceptance by many firms of flexible working time arrangements.

In terms of flexibility in numbers the concept of a core workforce has become more of a reality now. This in part links in with the idea of multi-skilled employees, who are essential for the core workforce to be effective. The real value to the company of flexibility in numbers comes from being able to use part-time, temporary and subcontract employees at times of peak capacity.

Essentially the idea behind all of these changes has been to allow the firm to achieve flexibility in its labour costs and arrangements to match the demand for its products or services. The CBI's own research indicates that within the period 1980-85, 60 per cent of manufacturing firms had gained some concessions during bargaining related to changes in working practices or arrangements.

Three further issues which have arisen during collective bargaining have been longer-term and single-union agreements, and no-strike deals. These have been accepted by certain unions, but on the whole they continue to be an uncommon feature of negotiations.

5. The climate of industrial relations: Disputes, co-operation and participation

The number of industrial disputes recorded in the United Kingdom has shown a secular decline since the mid-1970s, until a situation has been reached today where less than 2 per cent of plants in manufacturing are likely to have a dispute over pay in any one year. To confirm this trend, the number of working days lost each year due to strikes has been declining, though this was interrupted in 1979 by the "Winter of Discontent" and again in 1984 by the miners' strike. Any reputation that the United Kingdom may once have had as a "strike-prone" country is certainly not justifiable. In fact, industrial relations in business in the United Kingdom are very peaceful.

While there has clearly been a movement away from overt conflict, has this necessarily led to greater co-operation? Numerous studies have been undertaken to ascertain just how far employee involvement has progressed within firms, and what forms this involvement has taken. The results of these studies suggest that there has undoubtedly been a trend towards greater co-operation, as managers and employees both recognise that in order to restore competitiveness, and thus ensure continued operation, more co-operative industrial relations are essential.

The structures used for communications have not changed drastically. Rather, they have been used more effectively and have been extended in to new areas. Joint consultation bodies continue to be important arenas in which formal discussions can take place between management and representatives of employees. However, the real area of growth is in terms if informal two-way communications. Team briefings provide the opportunities for both employers and employees to voice their concerns over matters of work, as do "quality circles". Similarly many larger firms have revamped their company publications, and introduced other forms of communication such as video presentations. Alongside all such formal structures and arrangements are a host of informal ad hoc arrangements to inform employees of developments and future plans and to gather their views. The central theme behind all of these changes is the need to generate a sense of common commitment, with all those working in a company having a shared interest in its success and prosperity.

In this context, the rapid spread of employee shareholding schemes, backed by tax incentives, has been a major feature of the 1980s. Many publicly quoted companies now operate profit-sharing and/or share-option schemes, providing equity holdings for employees on highly advantageous terms. Many other firms have experimented with cash-based schemes related to company fortunes, based on profits, value added, return on capital or other measures of performance.

The Government has provided tax incentives to encourage the spread of employee share ownership. More recently, in the 1987 Finance Act, tax concessions have been introduced to encourage firms to adopt Profit Related Pay schemes which link part of base pay to profits. The rationale behind this move, however, was not only to increase co-operation; it was also to increase flexibility within the economy, so that pay and not numbers employed change when a firm's profitability is reduced. It is expected that there will be a significant number of companies who will move towards this form of employee remuneration.

6. Conclusion

In the 1980s there have been significant changes in industrial relations practices. Most notably, the difficulties and conflicts of the 1970s have been replaced by a period of co-operation and rapid improvement in productivity. The ever-increasing competitive pressures have led to a far greater attention to non-price competitiveness, this being possible only because of the more realistic approach now being adopted by employers and employees alike. It is highly likely that this favourable trend towards co-operation and the resultant improvement in economic performance will continue into the future, as the competitive pressures which initially brought it about are unlikely to diminsh.

It is against this background that collective bargaining has been undertaken, which has allowed many favourable changes to be made. The varied approaches to relating reward more closely to performance which have characterised pay bargaining have been a positive move which is likely to continue into the future. Recent innovations in bargaining, such as no-strike deals, single-union and long-term agreements, combined with the general move towards greater flexibility, are an important step in the direction of improved efficiency and competitiveness which will have to be taken further in the years ahead.

Collective bargaining in the United States: Recent trends and problems

H.C. Spring, Executive Assistant to the Deputy Under Secretary for
Labor-Management Relations and Co-operative Programs

1. Introduction

In the industrial relations arena during 1987, both unions and employers adopted innovative bargaining techniques to meet new and intricate problems. The growth of a global economy and technological innovation continued to change the infrastructure of American industrial relations. While the collective bargaining process saw great advance in labour-management co-operation, it also experienced some bitter disputes that seemed more typical of the adversarial atmosphere of labour relations that prevailed in the turbulent 1930s.

With the exception of the automobile industry, the trend away from pattern bargaining continued. Union leaders, though concerned about economic gains, focused attention on issues other than traditional wage demands, such as job security and retraining for dislocated members. Lump-sum payments in lieu of across-the-board wage increases, restrictions on plant closures, and limitations on outsourcing are common to many recently negotiated collective bargaining contracts. Employers, however, placed priority on reducing labour costs.

2. Collective bargaining: Substance

In 1986-87, major negotiations took place in the aerospace, airline, longshore, telephone, television and motion picture, and meatpacking industries. Particular attention focused on both the automobile and steel industries as well, not only because of their role in the overall economic health of the nation but for the significant changes in the process and results of their bargaining, as discussed in more detail below.

Wage settlements, as in previous years, provided for smaller increases and collective bargaining contracts were often concessionary. The Bureau of Labor Statistics reported that wage adjustments under major collective bargaining settlements during the first nine months of 1987 averaged 2.1 per cent in the first year of a negotiated contract and 2.3 per cent annually over the life of the contract. Adjustments during 1986 averaged 1.2 per cent in the first contract year and 1.8 per cent annually over the life of the contract. These settlements reflected continued employer preference to "backload" contracts (i.e. provide lower increases in the first year of multi-year contracts). In 1986, for the third consecutive year, non-union workers in the private sector received higher percentages of wage and benefit increases than their union counterparts.

3. Collective bargaining: Climate

The industrial relations panorama in 1986-87 contained several notable events. The US Postal Service concluded agreements with the American Postal Workers' Union and National Association of Letter Carriers (representing 540,000 postal employees) under provisions of the Postal Reorganization Act of 1970, which prohibits work stoppages. In the event of a bargaining impasse, the law mandates a procedure beginning with fact-finding and ending, if necessary, with arbitration. But the two unions reached agreement with the Postal Service, with the assistance of the Federal Mediation and Conciliation Service and without the need for arbitration, on 21 July 1987, the date of expiration of the old contract. (A third union, the Mail Handlers Division of the Laborers' International Union, representing 50,000 workers, settled separately.)

Bargaining in the steel industry also warranted special attention. Nation-wide bargaining in steel broke down during the mid-1980s, and was replaced by company-by-company bargaining (at Armco Steel, negotiations were conducted on a plant-by-plant basis). Almost all steel-producing companies demanded and received wage and benefit concessions in strike-free negotiations prior to the 184-day work stoppage – called a strike by most industry sources and a lock-out by unions – involving the United Steel Workers of America (USWA) and USX Corporation, formerly known as US Steel. This dispute was the longest major work stoppage in the history of the steel industry, beginning on 31 July 1986 (at midnight) and ending with ratification of a concessionary contract on 31 January 1987.

The USX contract has a four-year duration, which the USWA agreed to in return for company commitments to modernise facilities. This provides USX with a contract which will continue 18 months after those with other major steel firms expire. The USX pact (1 February 1987-31 January 1991) covers 22,000 active and 11,000 laid-off workers.

Negotiations in the automobile industry were just as intense but less turbulent. Contracts between the United Auto Workers and both Ford and General Motors expired on 14 September 1987. Long before expiration, the union had cited job security for the 104,000 hourly employees at Ford and 335,000 workers at GM as the focal issue for bargaining. The UAW named Ford as a possible strike target based on many factors, but essentially on Ford's economic strength in comparison with GM's.

On 17 September 1987, the Ford-UAW talks concluded with an agreement after a marathon 30-hour bargaining session. The company agreed to a 3 per cent wage increase in the first year and 3 per cent lump-sum bonuses (not added to base wage rates) in each of the following years, plus continuation of cost-of-living allowances. The key to the contract, however, was the Guaranteed Employment Numbers (GEN) provision. Under GEN, all Ford employees have their jobs guaranteed; temporary lay-offs would be allowed only in the event of a sales slump, and the company's right to eliminate jobs through attrition would be severely restricted. Ford also agreed to continue the plant-closing moratorium contained in the 1984 contract, and is barred from extending temporary lay-offs by reason of outsourcing or productivity improvements through new technology. Ford Motor Company officials called the contract "historic", and the UAW concurred. (Rank-and-file ratification occurred on 30 September, with a 72 per cent approval rating.)

The UAW extended the contract provisions of the 1984 pact on a day-to-day basis while bargaining with Ford, and all but suspended negotiations with GM during the interim. When negotiations with GM resumed, the union set no strike date. Statements from GM personnel that some settlement similar to Ford's could be reached and harmonious labour-management relations over the past few years played a significant role in the UAW decision. In fact, GM and the UAW reached tentative agreement on 8 October. The agreement was, basically, a pattern settlement, adopting job security provisions, health and safety benefits, and an enhanced profit-sharing formula similar to those at Ford. Job security guarantees and the moratorium on plant closings did not extend to those plants slated for closing before negotiations commenced.

Chrysler Corporation, which purchased American Motors and assumed its labour contracts, will bargain with the United Auto Workers next year; its contract expires in September 1988. In other developments, workers at Japan's Mazda car facility in Flat Rock, Michigan, voted overwhelmingly for UAW representation in September 1987; the Ford Motor Company owns considerable shares of Mazda and many experts feel this played an important role in the recognition process. In contrast to that successful organising drive, the UAW postponed indefinitely plans for a representational election at Honda Motor Company operations in Ohio.

It is also important to note that the automobile industry, probably more than any other in the United States, has adopted labour-management co-operation to compete with economic and environmental forces instead of adversarialism. Ford's Employee Involvement Program and GM's Saturn and NUMMI projects are noteworthy examples of this co-operation, as are the tremendous joint efforts aimed at training and retraining workers.

As in the automobile industry, job security and economic security have become priorities for many unions. The Communications Workers and Electrical Workers (IBEW) negotiating in 1986 in a deregulated communications industry that has had some employment decline, focused on job security provisions and formed a "new alliance" for training workers. In early 1987, the United Mine Workers and Island Creek Coal Corporation agreed to an "Employment and Economic Security Pact" (EESP) providing employees with first opportunity rights for jobs at all company operations, including newly acquired or opened mines. The pact requires subcontractors to meet UMW labour standards and offer employment to laid-off Island Creek employees. The union agreed not to strike the company at the expiration of the current national wage agreement (February 1988), and the company agreed to sign the successor to that agreement. Statements by both union and management on the EESP emphasised the co-operative nature of their relationship, and noted their agreement to jointly administer educational and improved communications programmes. Island Creek is the 13th largest coal producer, a subsidiary of Occidental Petroleum. It separated from the major coal employers' association in 1984 prior to contract bargaining, but accepted "me too" arrangements for that contract.

Bargaining by the UAW with Ford and GM in 1987 marked the first time negotiations took place without the union's Canadian locals, which seceded to form a separate union in 1986 (one Ontario local remains in the UAW). Some lumber worker unions on the Pacific Coast also split into separate American and Canadian entities, a move also indicative of the effects of nationalist sentiment on the structure of heretofore "international" unions.

The trade union movement as a whole has also been affected by many economic and environmental forces. Unions in the maritime, airline, electrical, communications and energy industries discussed or consummated mergers during the year; newspaper and graphic workers formulated plans for co-ordinated bargaining. Of interest too was the announcement by the independent United Mine Workers of its intent to explore merger possibilities with several AFL-CIO affiliates – the steel workers, electrical workers, and oil, chemical and atomic workers. The International Brotherhood of Teamsters, with about 1.6 million members, has rejoined the AFL-CIO after a 30-year absence.

In addition, some unions demonstrated signs of resurgence. Air traffic controllers, without a union following the 1981 controllers' strike, formed the National Air Traffic Controllers Association, affiliated, as was PATCO, its predecessor, with the Marine Engineers Beneficial Association.

Since the 1970s, union membership as a percentage of the workforce has declined precipitously, but in the last two years the rate of decline has stabilised. The Bureau of Labor Statistics has estimated that over the last two years about 17.5 per cent of all workers in the United States belonged to a labour organisation. AFL-CIO president Lane Kirkland claims that the deceleration trend is now reversing. Among the fastest growing organisations are those in the service industries and the public sector, including the United Food and Commercial Workers, the Service Employees International Union, and the American Federation of State, County and Municipal Employees.

4. *Employer responses*

Although many major firms (e.g. Xerox, General Motors, ALCOA) have embraced co-operative labour-management relations to improve their operations, some employers are more aggressive in dealing with unions and are attempting to convince them that labour costs must remain low to compete in a non-union and global market-place. For example, a survey of some 215 firms by a private research group indicates that payment of lump sums in lieu of general wage increases and adoption of two-tier wage systems have continued to be popular among employers.

Employer resistance to union demands is represented by their increasing commitment to replacing striking workers, an apparent trend with growing implications for the collective bargaining process. Seventy-seven per cent of employers recently polled indicated that, if a strike took place, they would attempt to replace their workforce or consider such action to keep operating. In 1985 Geo. A. Hormel & Co., a leading meat packer, engaged local P-9 of the United Food and Commercial Workers in Minnesota in a one-year strike/lock-out that included replacement of strikers and the virtual destruction of the local union. The meat packing industry, in general, adopted the tactic of replacing striking workers: in 1987, the Iowa Beef Processing Co., John Morrell Co., and Patrick Cudahy Co., all threatened to replace strikers or consummated those threats during disputes. Both Trans World Airlines and Boise Cascade, a paper products company, engaged in striker replacement practices. The replacement of striking football players by National Football League owners was perhaps the example of such an activity most visible to the general public.

5. Role of the State

The federal Government plays a very limited role in the collective bargaining process. The United States has no judicial body specifically designed to control aspects of industrial relations – the National Labor Relations Board is a quasi-judicial body that monitors and conducts representation elections and oversees the collective bargaining process. With the exception of certain strikes that jeopardise public safety and welfare, giving the Government the authority to intervene through the Taft-Hartley Act of 1947, the Government by statute allows disputing parties in the private sector to resolve their own differences. Mediation services, of course, are proffered through the Federal Mediation and Conciliation Service (FMCS).

There are, however, some exceptions to this policy. Under the Railway Labor Act (RLA) of 1926, amended as recently as 1981, the federal Government can act to delay work stoppages in the railroad and airline industries. If the emergency provisions of the RLA are invoked by the President, workers can be kept on the job for a 60-day "cooling-off" period while fact-finding by an impartial panel takes place. Moreover, in disputes involving rail commuter service lines, the cooling-off periods extend for up to 240 days, and the procedures must be invoked if requested by either party to the dispute or the governor of a directly affected state. In January 1987, after cooling-off periods had expired and a strike had begun on the Long Island (commuter) Railroad, Congress enacted ad hoc legislation to prohibit strike action for 60 days, during which the dispute was resolved.

The Railway Labor Act also allows workers in transportation industries to engage in some activities that are prohibited for other workers. In fact, the activity of "secondary picketing" (i.e. union members working for another railroad line can picket the centralised rail yards, where all lines converge and use the same trackage, thus encouraging other union members not to cross those lines) is currently a controversial issue in the dispute between the workers and new owners of the Pittsburgh and Lake Erie Railroad. In 1986, during a strike by the Brotherhood of Maintenance of Way Employees against the Boston and Maine Railroad, owned by Guilford Transportation industries, picket lines sprang up along the eastern seaboard, threatening to immobilise much of the nation's rail system. In early 1987 the challenge by the Burlington Northern and other railroads to the legality of the union action was rejected by the United States Supreme Court.

6. Role of the Department of Labor

The Department of Labor, through its Bureau of Labor-Management Relations and Co-operative Programs, promotes co-operative labour-management efforts in order to enhance the quality of working life while improving the productivity and competitiveness of American industry. To this end, it sponsors or conducts research, seminars, information-sharing, and training about co-operation and publishes information materials on related subjects. The Bureau recently ventured into the video age with the production of the documentary film "Work Worth Doing". The Bureau has been increasingly involved in international co-operation on productivity and QWL, as evidenced by its co-sponsorship of the International Productivity Symposium III in Washington in April 1988.

Despite the shared desires of some employers and their workers to adopt worker participation plans suited to the needs of their particular enterprises, it is not altogether clear that these new co-operative arrangements fit within the framework of the existing labour relations structure, which seems to reward confrontation over co-operation, and which has been widely characterised as rule driven and adversarial.

These concerns have led the Department of Labor to embark on a study of the nation's labour and related laws that may impede improvements in labour-management relations. The intent of this study, which has come to be known as the "Laws Project", is to produce information that can assist labour and management to reach consensus on whether the laws need to be made more hospitable to experiments in co-operation. The rationale for the Government's undertaking this inquiry is that, in our view, government should provide laws that clearly delineate between lawful and unlawful actions and that permit the parties to work together, without undue fear of legal challenge, to solve mutual problems and meet mutual needs.

The Laws Project was launched in June 1986 under the direction of then Deputy Under Secretary Stephen I. Schlossberg (Mr. Schlossberg is now Director of the ILO Branch Office, Washington, DC) with the issuance of a paper setting forth areas for possible inquiry. Subsequent reports have included research and discussion pieces on issues such as the effect of certain National Labor Relations Board and court decisions under the NLRA on the adoption of co-operative mechanisms. The First Interim Report discussed court and NLRB decisions on whether employee involvement groups such as quality circles may meet the definition of a labour organisation under the Act and whether employer creation of or support for such arrangements may run afoul of the prohibitions on employer domination, interference or support. The report concluded that co-operation may be compatible with the restrictions of the NLRA if, for example, employee involvement groups do not play the "representative" function traditionally carried out by a labour organisation, or if employer actions are not aimed at either undermining or supporting a union's position.

The Second Interim Report contains an extensive discussion of legal impediments to co-operation in the federal service and a review of the interplay between the NLRA's duty of fair representation and the changing role of unions in co-operative mechanisms. Another issue examined in the Laws Project is the potential effect on employee involvement generally of the United States Supreme Court's 1980 decision in *NLRB v. Yeshiva University*. In that case the court found that faculty members at the institution had so much input into management decisions that they were "in effect, substantially and pervasively operating the enterprise". Accordingly, faculty members were held to be managerial employees not entitled to the protections of the NLRA.

The *Yeshiva* decision and most subsequent related ones have arisen in the context of professional workers. Concerns have been expressed, however, whether blue-collar workers may also be vulnerable to the loss of bargaining rights because they have too much input into management decisions or too much say in how their work is performed. It is gratifying to note some preliminary indications that the rationale of *Yeshiva* may not necessarily be extended to the blue-collar workforce, and that the sharing of power that flows from co-operation does not automatically trigger the application of the supervisory or managerial exclusion.

In a recent decision, for example, the NLRB weighed the application of the NLRA's definition of "supervisor" to the relationship of production employees working in a team headed by a team leader. The statutory requisites for supervisory status include factors such as the power to "assign", "reward", "discipline" or "responsibility to direct" employees. Although the "teams as a whole routinely participate in decision-making regarding such personnel functions as discipline, job and overtime assignments, and performance efficiency appraisals ..." the Board declined to exclude team leaders from he bargaining unit. Acknowledging that the "team concept" of work organisation is a "novel and rather complex conceptual framework ... which was surely not contemplated by the drafters of the Act over 50 years ago ..." the Board endorsed its Regional Director's finding that the team leaders "function primarily as spokespersons on behalf of their respective team" and "do not ... possess or exercise supervisory authority on an independent basis in furtherance of management's interest ...".

Ongoing areas of inquiry in the project include the effects of the Railway Labor Act on co-operation and impediments to co-operation in state and local Government. It is clear that the Laws Project has succeeded in stimulating research into and discussion of the relationship between co-operation and the law. As the Department looks toward winding up its involvement in the Laws Project by the end of 1988, it is hoped that discussions, dialogue and research by and among interested persons will continue.

Collective bargaining in the United States: Recent trends and problems

O.M. Sherman, Retired Vice-President, Goodyear Tyre and Rubber Company

Some preliminary comments may be of help in evaluating my view of collective bargaining in the United states as it has evolved over the last 15 years. *First,* having retired from active participation in bargaining seven years ago, my views do not represent a particular company or an industry. Whether my views are more objective than those of an active participant can be argued about, of course, but I can look on current activities with a good deal of dispassion. Also, time has a way of providing a degree of clarity to, and understanding of, past events that is not present at the time of occurrence. *Second,* as the academic leader of an annual seminar on labour relations sponsored by the Labor Policy Association of Washington DC, I keep in touch with current activities and developments. The chief personnel officers of a dozen major corporations participate in the seminar, and extensive consultations, including the preparation of written cases for discussion during the seminar, are held with them. In the course of the seminar I am called upon to comment on various cases, all of which deal with real current situations, and to lead discussions on the broader significance of the developments.

Collective bargaining in the United States has been influenced by a variety of factors in the last 15 years, and there have been significant changes in the nature of bargaining, the subjects of bargaining and the locus of bargaining. Furthermore, the effect of major company bargaining results on national wage scales and other employment conditions has lessened considerably. Some may feel that collective bargaining is not as important as in the past, but this is arguable.

The major factor influencing collective bargaining in the United States was, and continues to be, world-wide markets and competition. Other factors of considerable importance are technological changes in both product and process, inflation and composition of the workforce, particularly the employment of women. Some may credit the increased effectiveness of employers in avoiding unionisation with a major role, but it can also be argued that this development is in large measure in response to competition, as well as the opportunity presented by technological change.

Unconcerned about foreign competition, major companies and the unions representing their employees in years past engaged in pattern bargaining, in which the great majority, if not all, of the producers of a particular commodity accepted the same economic settlement, virtually assuring themselves of comparatively equal labour costs. Over the years this resulted in a significant degree of structured rigidity in both companies and the unions they bargained with. Costly and inefficient procedures and work practices were continued because the resistance to change was so great that a disproportionate effort was needed to effect change. Production costs were thus affected by both unemployment costs and employee productivity.

The availability of high-quality, lower-priced imported products in the United States market resulted in extreme pressure on the bargaining relationship between United States companies and the unions representing their employees, and continues to be a major influence on current bargaining. Companies have had to lower costs by whatever means were available. The development that has had the most effect in convincing employees and their unions that changes must be accepted has been the job loss resulting from decreased market share and the discontinuance of inefficient operations. In many cases companies replaced these inefficient operations with new facilities utilising newly available production technology, and undertook successful efforts to avoid union organisation of the employees in these facilities. The argument for the latter was greater employee flexibility and performance. Recourse to foreign production facilities also resulted in lost jobs.

Unionised employees as a percentage of the total workforce have declined significantly in recent years, not only because of the dislocation caused by foreign competition, but also because of the shift from manufacturing to so-called service industries represented in large measure by smaller employers, reputedly more difficult to organise. Most of the job growth has occurred in small businesses, where efforts to organise workers are both expensive and troublesome from a structural standpoint.

Faced with today's realities both employers and unions come to the bargaining table with different agendas from those that were the case previously. Bargaining strategies have also changed. The decisions are undoubtedly more difficult for the unions than the employers, given the necessity of obtaining the consent of at least a majority of the employees to any changes in wages, benefits and working conditions. Whereas union demands for increases in wages and benefits used to be the norm, unions' efforts are now directed towards preserving pay scales and preserving jobs. Job security issues have risen to the top of the bargaining agenda, matched on the employers' side by strong arguments for changes in employment procedures and work rules.

In large-company, multi-plant bargaining the work rule issue has very often resulted in increased involvement of plant-level unions in the overall economic settlement. Work rules usually vary from plant to plant, for one thing, and obtaining employee assent to changes is made easier by the direct contact they have with their union representatives and the plant management. An outgrowth of this development has been a significant increase in the amount and nature of information on company financial performance that is provided to employees and their unions.

Pattern bargaining has declined perceptibly as the parties have had to recognise that the cost problems of all companies cannot be resolved in the same way. This has put a strain on the national unions, which not only have to deal with each company separately, but have to accede to the fact that some of their bargaining authority has transferred to the plant-level unions – all this at a time when national union resources are limited and often reduced by declines in dues-paying members.

The discontinuance of operations and plant closures have served to support employer arguments for reductions in nominal levels of compensation and far less restrictive procedures and work rules. Corporate bargaining strategy can be based effectively on the implied or even explicit possibility of job losses should satisfactory agreement on changes not be achieved. This strategy has had the effect of reducing the threat of a strike, since striking employees have to face the likelihood that there will be no jobs to come back to after the strike is over.

On the other hand, the possibility of job losses has given the unions an important bargaining issue and remarkable ingenuity has been demonstrated in bargained arrangements to accommodate employee concerns. Agreements variously provide for extended periods of notice of impending lay-offs and discontinuance of operations, employment rights in other company operations, retraining and re-employment assistance, severance pay and early retirement programmes, as well as guarantees of continued employment for specific periods. Unions have also bargained for extended consultation on various matters affecting employment, both directly and indirectly, including production planning and outsourcing of products. The protection of retirement benefits has received considerable attention, made important by the decreasing ratio of active employees to the retired population.

In some cases, companies and unions have participated in co-operative efforts that are remarkable by previous standards. To some degree these efforts have improved performance, as well as the relations between companies and unions, particularly at the plant level. Whether these understandings will stand the test of time and changing fortunes remains to be seen.

Companies and unions, as would be expected, have not been uniformly successful in arriving at satisfactory arrangements to relieve company concerns about production costs and union and employee concerns about employment and income security. Many companies, particularly smaller ones, either have not the resources to provide unemployment security measures or do not have sufficient control of their activities to undertake such arrangements. In a number of cases the *quid pro quo* has not been reached and both companies and employees have suffered severe dislocations.

The twin transitions from national markets to international markets and the shift in employment from the manufacturing sector to the service sector have resulted in large-scale dislocations in employment. Although total employment in the country is high, and unemployment is at a low point in this decade, large numbers of people have had to accept involuntary changes in jobs, sometimes in different locations and without assistance of any kind from their previous employers.

Concerned with the relatively large number of employees whose employers provide little or no advance notice or assistance in the event of job discontinuance, either temporary or permanent, the national unions are supporting efforts at the federal level, as well as the state level, to legislate such provisions. As expected, employer associations are resisting these efforts. Thus, in a real sense, collective bargaining has shifted from the private bargaining table to the public. It should be noted that these efforts have been made part of broader proposals dealing with international trade, some of which are supported in part by employers.

Another development which has had a significant impact on collective bargaining should be mentioned. Previously regulated industries, particularly airlines and telecommunications, found themselves in different competitive circumstances when they became subject to market forces. When competition puts pressure on costs, the effect on collective bargaining in these industries is very similar to that experienced by those industries affected by world-wide market forces.

It is interesting that unions have had the most success in recent years, both in their organising efforts and in the results of collective bargaining, in the public sector. While governments are subject to the restraints of limited resources as opposed to the demand for increased services, the competitive pressures provided by alternative providers do not exist to anywhere near the same degree.

Like most other institutions in a free society, collective bargaining is a dynamic process, and I believe it is alive and well in the United States, even if it is imperfect. Most thinking employers, not necessarily a majority, will agree that in a free society, employees should have the right to join a union, should they believe it is in their interest to be so represented. At the same time, many of these same thinking employers would prefer not to have to deal with a union. Thus it is incumbent on them to manage employee relations accordingly, whatever that may involve in their particular situation. In this sense, collective bargaining serves most of those people who work for a living, whether they are represented or not.

Appendix. List of participants and observers

A. Participants

Australia

Mr. Bill MANSFIELD
Assistant-Secretary
Australian Council of Trade Unions
ACTU House
393 Swanston Street
MELBOURNE 3000

Mr. Bryan M. NOAKES
Director General
Confederation of Australian Industry
National Employers Industrial Council (CAI)
44th Level, Nauru House
80 Collins Street
MELBOURNE – VICTORIA 3000

Mr. Douglas POULTER
Special Labour Adviser
Permanent Mission of Australia to the Office
   of the United Nations
56-58 rue de Moillebeau
Petit Saconnex
1211 GENÈVE (Suisse)

Mr. Bernard YATES
Principal Adviser
Wages and Incomes Policy
Department of Industrial Relations
1, Farrell Place
CANBERRA ACT. 2601

Austria

Dr. Max ARBESSER-RASTBURG
Prokurist
Linke Wienzeile 18
A-1060 WIEN

Mr. Helmut BRAND
Gewekschaft der Privatangestellten
Deutschmeisterplatz 2
A-1010 WIEN

Dr. Erwin FISCHER
Leiter der Abteilung Arbeits- und Sozialrecht
Österreichischer Raiffeisenverband
Hollandstrasse 2
A-1020 WIEN

Dr. Richard LEUTNER
Sozialpolitischer Referent Osterreichischer
   Gewerkschaftsbund
Hohenstaufengasse 10-12
A-1010 WIEN

Mr. Wilhelm MOUTVITZ
Leiter des Rechtbüros
Gewerkschaft Metall-Bergbau Energie
Plösslgasse 15
A-1040 – WIEN

Dr. Bernhard SCHWARZ
Leiter der Sozialpolitischen Abteilung
Arbeiterkammer Wien
Prinz Eugen Strasse 20
A-1040 WIEN

Dr. Dietmar STRIMITZER
Referent der sozialpolitischen Abteilung der
   Bundeskammer der gewerblichen Wirtschaft
Wiedner Hauptstrasse 63 – Postfach 107
A-1045 WIEN

Dr. Thomas WIDORN
Abteilungsleiter
Bundesministerium für Arbeit und Soziales
Stubenring 1
A-1010 WIEN

Belgium

M. Roger BLANPAIN
Professeur
Institut du droit du travail
Katholieke Universiteit Leuven
Tiensestraat 41
B-3000 LEUVEN

Mr. Marcel BOURLARD
Professeur à l'Université de Louvain
Conseiller-Expert
Ministère de l'Emploi et du Travail
Rue Belliard 53
B-1040 BRUXELLES

M. M. DEFORT
Directeur général du service des relations collectives
Ministère de l'Emploi et du Travail
Rue Belliard 53
B-1040 BRUXELLES

M. Arnout DE KOSTER
Fédération des entreprises de Belgique
Rue Ravenstein 4
B-1000 BRUXELLES

M. Joseph SERVOTTE
Collaborateur au Service d'Etudes de la CSC
Section "Problèmes juridiques"
Confédération des Syndicats chrétiens
B-1040 BRUXELLES

M. STALPORT
Fédération générale des travailleurs de Belgique
Maison syndicale
42 rue Haute
B-1000 BRUXELLES

Canada

Mr. J.F. ALLISON
Vice-President Industrial Relations
Abitibi-Price Inc.
207 Queen's quay West
Suite 680, Box 102
TORONTO (Ontario) M5J 2P5

M. Robert DEAN
Représentant national
Travailleurs canadiens de l'automobile du Canada
7275 Sherbrooke est
Bureau 305
MONTREAL (Québec) H1N 1E9

M. Raymond DESILETS
Sous-ministre adjoint
Direction générale des relations du Travail
Ministère du Travail du Québec
255 est, boul. Crémazie, $11^{\text{ème}}$ étage
MONTRÉAL (Québec) H2M 1L5

Ms. Louise DOYON
Professeur
Département des sciences juridiques
Université du Québec à Montréal
4383 Melrose
MONTRÉAL (Québec) (H4A 2S7)

M. Gilles FERLAND
Professeur
Département des relations industrielles
Université Laval
C.P. 270
Ste MÉLANIE (Québec) (JOK 3A0)

M. Jean-Guy FRENETTE
Conseiller politique de la FTQ
Fédération des travailleurs du Québec (FTQ)
2100 Papineau, 4e étage
MONTRÉAL (Québec) (H2K 4J4)

Mme GAUTHIER-MONTPLAISIR
Avocate, Arbitre de grief
Case postale 270
STE MÉLANIE (Québec)

Mr. Ron LANG
Director of Policy and Planning/Research & Legislation
Canadian Labour Congress
2841 Riverside Drive
OTTAWA (Ontario) (K1V 8X7)

M. Robert MAHEU
Directeur du personnel
ALCAN ALUMINIUM s.a.
13, quai de l'Ile
1211 GENÈVE 11

Dr. Keith NEWTON
Senior Project Director
Economic Council of Canada
P.O. Box 527
OTTAWA (Ontario) (K1P5V6)

Mr. Victor PATHE
Assistant Deputy-Minister
Industrial Relations Division
Ministry of Labour of Ontario
400 University Avenue, 14th floor
TORONTO (Ontario) (M7A 1T7)

M. Claude RIOUX
Coordonnateur général des négociations (secteur privé)
Confédération des syndicats nationaux
1601 avenue de Lorimier
MONTRÉAL (Québec) (H2K 4M5)

Cyprus

    M. Nelson NEOCLEUS
    Senior Labour Officer (Industrial Relations)
    Ministry of Labour and Social Insurance
    NICOSIA

    Mr. Michael PILIKOS
    Industrial Relations Officer
    Cyprus Employers and Industrialists Federation (OEB)
    P.O. Box 1657
    NICOSIA

Denmark

    Mr. Henrik Marstrand DAHL
    Head of Division
    Danish Employers' Confederation
    Vester Voldgade 113
    DK-1503 COPENHAGEN V

    Mr. Einar EDELBERG
    Head of Division
    Ministry of Labour
    19 Laksegade
    DK-1063 COPENHAGEN K

    Mr. Poul JORNING
    Head of Division
    Danish Federation of Public Servants'
    and Salaried Employees' Organisations
    (Funktionaerernes og Tjenestemaendenes Fabllesrad
      (FTF))
    Niels Hemmingsensgade 12
    Post Box 1169
    DK-1010 COPENHAGEN K

    Ms. Elise Hammer KRISTENSEN
    Head of Section
    Ministry of Labour
    19 Laksegade
    DK-1063 COPENHAGEN K

    Mr. Knud Mols SORENSEN
    Vice President
    Salaried Employees' and Civil Servants' Confederation
      (FTF-DK)
    Dansk Styrmandsforening
    Havnegade 55
    DK-1058 COPENHAGEN K

Finland

Mr. Teuvo KALLIO
National Conciliation Officer
Ministry of Social Affairs and Health
Bulevardi 6 A
SF-00120 HELSINKI

Mr. Ismo LUIMULA
Economist
The Central Organisation of Finnish Trade Unions
(Suomen Ammattiliittojen Keskusjärjestö SAK)
P.O. Box 161
SF-00531 HELSINKI

Mr. Mauri MOREN
Managing Director
Employers' Association of Finnish Forest Industries
(Metsäteollisuuden Keskusliitto)
Fabianinkatu 9 A
SF-00130 HELSINKI

Mr. Paavo J. PAAVOLA
Director
The Local Authorities' Negotiating Commission
(Kunnallisen sopimusvaltuuskunnan toimisto)
Toinen linja 14
SF-00530 HELSINKI

Mrs. Kirsti PALANKO-LAAKA
Head of the Legal Department
The Central Organisation of Finnish Trade Unions
(Suomen Ammattiliittojen Keskusjärjesto SAK)
P.O. Box 161
SF-00531 HELSINKI

Mr. Martti Olavi REUNA
Chief Negotiator
Confederation of Technical Employee Organisations
  in Finland
(Suomen Teknisten Toimihenkilöjärjestöjen
  Keskusliitto STTK)
Pohjoisranta 4 A
SF-00170 HELSINKI

Mr. Seppo RISKI
Director, Master of Laws
The Finnish Employers' Confederation
(Suomen Työnantajain Keskusliitto STK)
P.O. Box 30
SF-00131 HELSINKI

Mr. Antti Lauri Johannes TUOMI
Chief Negotiator
Confederation of Unions for Academic Professionals
   in Finland (AKAVA)
Rautatieläisenkatu 6
SF-00520 HELSINKI

Mr. Timo K. VERTANEN
Chief of Department
The Confederation of Salaried Employees (TVK)
Asemamiehenkatu 4
SF-00520 HELSINKI

France

M. Manuel BAMBERGER
Chef du Bureau des Conventions collectives et Conflits
   du Travail
Ministère des Affaires sociales et de l'Emploi
1 Place de Fontenoy
F-75700 PARIS

M. Yves DELAMOTTE
Professeur
Conservatoire national des Arts et Métiers (CNAM)
2, rue Conté
75003 PARIS

Mme Paulette HOFMANN
Secrétaire Confédéral
Confédération Force ouvrière (CGT-FO)
198 avenue du Maine
75014 PARIS

M. Thierry LAFONT
Adjoint au Directeur des questions sociales internationales
Conseil national du Patronat français
31 avenue Pierre 1er de Serbie
75016 PARIS

M. Jean-Marie NATHAN-HUDSON
Directeur des relations industrielles et humaines
   PEUGEOT s.a.
75 avenue de la Grande Armée
75117 PARIS

M. Roger PASCRÉ
Membre CGT de la Commission nationale de la
   négociation collective
Confédération générale du Travail
263 rue de Paris
F-93516 MONTREUIL (Cedex)

Germany, Federal Republic of

Dr. Klaus DUTTI
Hauptgeschäftsführer
Arbeitgeberverband des Privaten Bankgewerbes e.v.
Postfach 100104
5000 - KÖLN 51

Dr. Dieter GLEICHFELD
Deutsche Angestellten Gewerkschaft
Karl-Muck Platz, 1
2000 - HAMBURG 36

Dr. Peter KNEVELS
Geschäftsführer
Bundesvereinigung der Deutschen Arbeitgeberverbände
Gustav-Heinemann-Ufer, 72
5000 - KÖLN 51

Mr. Wolfgang KOBERSKI
Abteilung Arbeitsrecht im Bundesministerium für
  Arbeit und Sozialordnung
Postfach 140280
5300 - BONN 1

Mr. Joachim KREIMER DE FRIES
Referatsleiter
DGB Bundesvorstand
Postfach 2601
4000 - DÜSSELDORF 1

Greece

Mr. Nikolas ANALYTIS
Member of the Board,
Federation of Greek Industries
5 Xenophontos Street
GR-ATHENS 105 57

M. Emmanuel STRATAKIS
Attaché du travail
Consulat général de Grèce
Muhlebachstrasse 44
8008 ZÜRICH

Ireland

Mr. John BIGGAR
Permanent mission of Ireland to the UN
45-47 rue de Lausanne
1201 GENÈVE

Mr. D.J. McAULEY
Director-General
Federated Union of Employers
Baggot Bridge House
34, Lower Baggot Street
DUBLIN 2

Israel

Dr. Ozer CARMI
Directeur de l'Institut pour la promotion des relations
  professionnelles
P.O. Box 33010
IL-61330 TEL AVIV

Mr. Samuel GRUNSPAN
Histadrut Institute for Economic and Social Research
P.O. Box 303
TEL AVIV

Mr. Josef HAUSMANN
Labour Adviser
Manufacturers' Association of Israel
P.O. Box 500 22
TEL AVIV 68125

Italy

M. Alfio NOCITO
Attaché
Mission permanente d'Italie auprès des organisations
  internationales
10 chemin de l'impératrice
1292 CHAMBÉSY (Suisse)

M. Giuseppe ROTUNDO
Mission permanente d'Italie auprès des organisations
  internationales
10 chemin de l'impératrice
1292 CHAMBÉSY (Suisse)

Dr. Fausto SABBATUCCI
Coordinatore del Dipartimento Industriale della
Confederazione Generale Italiana del Lavoro (CGIL)
Corso d'Italia, 25
I-00198 – ROMA

M. SARACENO
Unione Italiana del Lavoro
Via Lucullo, 6
I-00187 ROMA

Prof. Tiziano TREU
Ordinario di Diritto del Lavoro dell'Università di Pavia
Via Conca del Naviglio, 22
I-20123 MILANO

Japan

Mr. Izao FUJIWARA
Vice-President
Japanese Confederation of Labour (DOMEI)
Domei yu ai kaikano
2-20-12 Shiba
Minato-ku
TOKYO 105

Mr. Tadashi NAKAMURA
Assistant Minister for International Affairs
International Labour Affairs Division
Ministry of Labour
2-2 Kasumigaseki, 1-Chome
Chiyoda-ku
TOKYO

Mr. Toshio SUZUKI
Director
International Division
Japan Federation of Employers' Association
 (NIKKEIREN)
4-6 Marunouchi 1-chome
Chiyoda-ku
TOKYO 100

Mr. Hiroshi TSUJINO
President
Ryoka Light Metal Industries Ltd.
5-2, Marunouchi 2-chome
Chiyoda-ku
TOKYO 100

Mr. Yoichi YAMADA
Director
International Bureau
General Council of Trade Unions of Japan
 (SOHYO)
3-2-11 Kandasurugadai
Chiyoda-ku
TOKYO

Luxembourg

M. Armand BARNICH
Chef de département
Confédération syndicale indépendante (OGB-L)
Boîte postale 149
L-4002 ESCH/ALZETTE

M. Ernest DORNSEIFFER
Inspecteur principal au Ministère du Travail
26, rue Zithe
2910 LUXEMBOURG

M. Léon DRUCKER
Secrétaire de la Confédération luxembourgeoise
  des syndicats chrétiens (LCGB)
11, rue du Commerce
LUXEMBOURG

Netherlands

Mr. J.K. BOUT
Directeur Sociale Zaken (Director of the Department
  for Social Affairs)
Algemene Werkgeversvereniging (General Association
  of Employers)
P.O. Box 568
2003 RN HAARLEM

Mr. H.J. BROUWER
Director for Labour Relations
Directorate-General for Matters of General Policy
Ministry of Social Affairs and Employment
P.O. Box 20801 (Zeestraat 73)
2500 EV THE HAGUE

Miss Cornelie HAK
Head of the International Labour Affairs Division
Federation of Netherlands Industry
VNO, P.O. Box 93093
2509 AB THE HAGUE

Dr. M.J. HUISKAMP
Research Manager of the Social Economic Council
Bezuidenhoutseweg 60
2509 LK THE HAGUE

Mrs. L. KOOTSTRA
Directorate for Labour Relations
Conditions of Employment Section
Ministry of Social Affairs and Employment
P.O. Box 20801 (Zeestraat 73)
2500 EV THE HAGUE

Mr. J.W. VAN DEN BRAAK
Secretary for Social Affairs
Netherlands Employers Federation
Prinses Beatrixlaan 5
THE HAGUE

New Zealand

Mr. Robert John M. HILL
Director
Employment Policy Division
Department of Labour
Private Bag
WELLINGTON

Mr. Steve MARSHALL
Director of Advocacy
New Zealand Employers' Federation (Inc.)
P.O. Box 1786
WELLINGTON

Norway

Mr. Lars Chr. BERGE
Assistant Director-General
Norwegian Employers' Confederation
P.O. Box 6710 St 01av Plass
N-0130 OSLO 1

Mr. Per BRANNSTEN
Economist
The Norwegian Federation of Trade Unions
Youngs Gate, 11
N-0181 OSLO 1

Mr. Knut GROHOLT
Director General
Ministry of Local Government and Labour
Box 8112 Dep.
N-0032 OSLO 1

Mr. Yngve HAGENSEN
Secretary
The Norwegian Federation of Trade Unions
Youngs Gate, 11
N-OSLO 1

Mr. Reidar WEBSTER
Department State Mediator
Norwegian Government
Nedre Vollgate 10
N-0158 OSLO I

Portugal

Sra Maria Laura GASPAR
Directora de Serviços do Departamento de Estudos e Planeamento
Ministerio do Emprego e da Segurança social
Departamento de Estudos e Planeamento
Ava. Defensores de Chavez, 95-3º
1000 LISBOA

M. Manuel JORDÃO
Attaché (Affaires sociales et du travail),
Mission permanente du Portugal auprès de l'Office des Nations Unies
1, rue Richard Wagner
1202 GENÈVE (Suisse)

Sra. Maria Josefina LEITÃO
Chefe de Divisão da Regulamentação Colectiva de Trabalho
   da Direcção Geral do Trabalho
Ministerio do Emprego e Segurança social
14º andar – Salla 11
Praça de Londres
LISBOA

Sr. Fernando Manuel P. MARQUES
Assessor na area de politica salarial
Confederação Geral dos Trabalhadores Portugueses
Intersindical Nacional
Rua Victor Cordon 1/3
P-1294 LISBOA Cedex

Sra. Maria José MENESES SOUTO
Técnica da Divisão Geral de Regulamentação Colectiva de Trabalho
   da Direcção Geral do Trabalho
Ministerio do Emprego e Segurança social
14º andar – Salla 11
Praça de Londres
LISBOA

Sr. Antonio MINEIRO
Tecnico da Confederação da Industria Portuguesa
Avenida 5 de outubro 35-1o
P-1000 LISBOA

Sra. Maria do Rosário Pinto dos SANTOS
Ministerio do Emprego e Segurança social
14o andar – Salla 11
Praça de Londres
LISBOA

Sra. Maria do Conceição S.A. SOUSA
Técnica da Direcção Geral das Relações Colectivas de Trabalho
Ministerio do Emprego e Segurança social
14º andar – Salla 11
Praça de Londres
LISBOA

Spain

Don Mariano DIAZ MATEOS
Adjunto al secretario confederal de CCOO
Secretaría General de la Confederación Sindical de CC.OO.
Secretariado de Relaciones Internacionales y Emigración
Calle Fernández de la Hoz, 12
MADRID

Don Federico DURAN LOPEZ
Catedrático de Derecho del Trabajo de la Universidad de Córdoba
Facultad de Derecho
Universidad de Córdoba
CÓRDOBA

Don Francisco GONZALES DE LENA ALVAREZ
Subdirector General para la Negociación colectiva y las condiciones
    de Trabajo del Ministerio de Trabajo y Seguridad Social
Dirección General de Trabajo
Pío Baroja, 6
28009 – MADRID

Don Juan Miguel MENDOZA AIZPURUA
Miembro de Solidaridad de Trabajadores, ELA/STV
Apartado 971
SAN SEBASTIAN

Don R. Ruiz ORTEGA
Departamento de Relaciones Laborales de la CEOE
Diego de León, 50
MADRID

Don Sergio SANTILLAN
Miembro del Gabinete Técnico de UGT
Secretaría General de UGT
Departamento Internacional
Calle San Bernardo, 20
MADRID

Sweden

Mr. Lars Johan EKLUND
Legal Adviser
Ministry of Labour
S-103 33 STOCKHOLM

M. Nils ELVANDER
Professeur
The Swedish Council for Management and Work Life Issues
P.O. Box 5042
S-102 41 STOCKHOLM

Mr. Jan HAGBERG
Redistribution Policy Department
Swedish Trade Union Confederation (Landsorganisationen i Sverige)
S-103 33 STOCKHOLM

Mr. Bo HANSSON
Head of Section
The Federation of Swedish County Council (Landstingsförbundet)
Box 6606
S-113 84 STOCKHOLM

Mr. Ronald KALLSTROM
Assistant Head of Negotiations
The Central Organisation of Salaried Employees in Sweden
(Tjänstemännens Centralorganisation)
Box 12 069
S-102 22 STOCKHOLM

Mr. Ulf NILSSON
Director, Head of Negotiations
Swedish Employers' Confederation (Svenska Arbetsgivareföreningen, SAF)
S-103 30 STOCKHOLM

Mr. Claes Torsten STRATH
Head of Section
The Swedish Association of Local Authorities
    (Svenska kommunförbundet)
Hornsgatan, 15
S-116 47 STOCKHOLM

Switzerland

M. Markus BEER
Chef de la section droit collectif du travail
OFIAMT
Gurtengasse 3
3003 BERN

M. Benno HARDMEIER
Secrétaire de l'Union syndicale suisse
Case postale 64
3000 BERN 23

M. Xavier Schnyder de WARTENSEE
Secrétaire de l'ASM
Arbeitgeberverband schweizerischer
Maschinen und Metallindustrieller
Kirchenweg 4 Postfach
8032 ZÜRICH

Turkey

Mr. Tekin AKIN
Secretary-General
Petroleum Industry Workers' Trade Union (PETROL-IS)
Yildiz Posta. Cad.
Evren Sitesi D. Block
GAYRETTEPE/ISTANBUL

Mr. Dervis ALBAYRAK
Director,
External Relations Unit of the Workers' Trade Union
  Confederation of Turkey (TURK-IS)
Bayindir Sok. # 10
ANKARA

Mr. Talha ALTINBASAK
Vice-President
Turkish Textile Employers' Association
Visnezade Cami Meydani Efe Apt.
No. 2 D/10 Besiktas
80680 ISTANBUL

Mr. Turker ARSLAN
Deputy Secretary-General
Turkish Textile Employers' Association
Visnezade Cami Meydani Efe Apt.
No. 2/10 Besiktas
80680 ISTANBUL

Mr. Ahmet BOLUKBASI
Legal Adviser
Turkish Employers' Association of Metal Industries
Abidei Hurriyet Cad. Mecidiyekoy Yolu
Boydas Han No. 268 Kat 4-5 Sisli
80270 ISTANBUL

Mr. Algun CIFTER
Legal Adviser
Employers' Union of Turkey
Cekirge Cad. No.101 Intam Is Merkesi Kat.4 D.401
BURSA

APPENDIX

Mr. Oguz DEMIRALP
Counsellor
Permanent Mission of Turkey to the UN
28, chemin du Petit Saconnex
1211 GENÈVE 19

Mr. Bora ERSAL
Deputy Secretary-General
Turkish Textile Employers' Association,
Visnezade Cami Meydani Efe Apt.
No. 2/10 Besiktas
80680 ISTANBUL

Mr. Kazim GOZUM
General Finance Secretary
Railways Workers' Trade Union (DEMIRYOLU-IS)
Necatibey Cad. Sezenler
Sok. # 5
ANKARA

Mr. Bahattin GEZER
Secretary-General
General Mine Workers' Trade Union
(GENEL MADEN-IS)
Nizam Caddesi Okul
Sok # 6
ZONGULDAK

Mr. Ilhan GOCER
Deputy Secretary-General
Turkish Confederation of Employer Associations
Mesrutiyet Cad. 1/4-5
ANKARA

Mr. Mustafa KETENCI
General Finance Secretary
Banking and Insurance Workers' Trade Unions of Turkey
    (BASISEN)
Istiklal Cad. # 311 K.4
ISTANBUL

Mr. Rafet KOYLAN
Representative of the Marmara Regional
Office of the Mine Workers' Trade Union of Turkey
(T. MADEN-IS)
Milli Kuvuetler Caddesi
Yesil Yol Sok # 2
BAUKESIR

Mr. Emin KUL
Secretary General
Workers' Trade Union Confederation of Turkey
   (TURK-IS)
Bayindir Sok # 10
ANKARA

Mr. Hüseyin PEKIN
Counsellor (Labour Affairs)
Permanent Mission of Turkey to the UN Office
   in Geneva,
28, chemin du Petit Saconnex
1211 GENÈVE 19

Mr. Ekrem SAMI
Secretary-General
Mine Workers' Trade Union of Turkey
(T.MADEN-IS)
Strazburg Cad. # 7
ANKARA

Mr. Cetin SOYAK
Deputy President
Defence and related industries
Workers' Trade Union of Turkey (TURK HARB-IS)
Tnkilap Sok # 20
ANKARA

Mr. Nail TANRIVERDI
Ministry of Labour and Social Security
Deputy Director-General of the General Directorate
   of Labour
Calisma Vekâleti
ANKARA

Mr. Suleyman YAZIR
Ministry of Labour and Social Security
Research, Planning and Coordination Council
Head of the International Relations Unit
Calisma Vekâleti
ANKARA

Mr. Nihat YUKSEL
Director, Industrial Relations and Labour Administration
   Department
Bossa Ticaret ve sanayii Isletmeleri T.A.S.
Ilbey Günes Cad. No. 130 Karsiyaka
01079 ADANA

United Kingdom

Miss Ann MACKIE
OBE, FIPM
Employee Relations Adviser
Unilever UKCR Ltd.
Unilever House
Blackfriars
LONDON EC4P 4BQ

Mr. Neil MILLWARD
Principal Research Officer
Social Science Branch
Department of Employment
Steel House, 11 Tothill Street
LONDON SW1

United States

M. Everett KASSALOW
Professeur
Center for Labor Studies
School of Urban and Public Affairs
Carnegie Mellon University
PITTSBURGH, PA 15213-3890

Mr. Rudolph A. OSWALD
Director of the Economic Research Department
American Federation of Labor and Congress of Industrial
    Organisations (AFL/CIO)
815 Sixteenth Street N.W.
WASHINGTON, DC, 20006

Mr. O.M. SHERMAN
Retired Vice-President Industrial Relations of Goodyear Tire
    and Rubber Co.
3497 Iris Court
BOULDER (CO 80309)

Mr. Charles SPRING
Executive Assistant to the Deputy under Secretary for Labor-
    Management Relations and Cooperative Programs
U.S. Department of Labor
200, Constitution Avenue, N.W., Room S2203
WASHINGTON, DC, 20210

B. Observers

ORGANISATION FOR ECONOMIC CO-OPERATION
AND DEVELOPMENT (OECD)
2, rue André Pascal
75016 PARIS Cedex 16

M. Ronald Oliver CLARKE
Principal Administrator
Social Affairs and Industrial Relations Division

COMMISSION OF THE EUROPEAN COMMUNITIES
Rue de la Loi 200
B-1049 BRUXELLES

M. Gaetano ZINGONE
Administrateur principal

INTERNATIONAL ORGANISATION OF EMPLOYERS
28, Chemin de Joinville
1216 COINTRIN/GENÈVE

Ms. Jutta ULBRICHT
Executive Secretary

INTERNATIONAL CONFEDERATION OF FREE TRADE
UNIONS (ICFTU)
27-29 rue de la Coulouvrenière
CH-1204 GENÈVE

M. O. DE VRIES REILINGH
Director of the Geneva Office

M. E. LAURIJSSEN
Assistant Director of the Geneva Office

WORLD CONFEDERATION OF LABOUR
1, rue Varembé
CH-1211 GENÈVE 20 CIC

M. Blaise ROBEL
Représentant permanent

Mme Béatrice FAUCHÈRE
Bureau de Genève

WORLD FEDERATION OF TRADE UNIONS
10, rue Fendt
1201 GENÈVE

M. Lucien LABRUNE
Représentant permanent

M. Ivan MITIAEV
Représentant permanent

www.ingramcontent.com/pod-product-compliance
Ingram Content Group UK Ltd.
Pitfield, Milton Keynes, MK11 3LW, UK
UKHW021320180426
11947UKWH00015B/1334